CRICUT
PROJECT IDEAS

Amanda Vinyl

AMANDA VINYL

© Copyright 2020 - All rights reserved.

The content contained within this book may not be reproduced, duplicated or transmitted without direct written permission from the author or the publisher.

Under no circumstances will any blame or legal responsibility be held against the publisher, or author, for any damages, reparation, or monetary loss due to the information contained within this book. Either directly or indirectly.

Legal Notice:

This book is copyright protected. This book is only for personal use. You cannot amend, distribute, sell, use, quote or paraphrase any part, or the content within this book, without the consent of the author or publisher.

Disclaimer Notice:

Please note the information contained within this document is for educational and entertainment purposes only. All effort has been executed to present accurate, up to date, and reliable, complete information. No warranties of any kind are declared or implied. Readers acknowledge that the author is not engaging in the rendering of legal, financial, medical or professional advice. The content within this book has been derived from various sources. Please consult a licensed professional before attempting any techniques outlined in this book.

By reading this document, the reader agrees that under no circumstances is the author responsible for any losses, direct or indirect, which are incurred as a result of the use of information contained within this document, including, but not limited to, errors, omissions, or inaccuracies.

Table of Contents

INTRODUCTION 8

CHAPTER 1: COMPONENTS OF THE CRICUT 12

    MODELS OVERVIEW 14

    WHICH CRICUT MODEL SHOULD YOU USE? 21

    TOOLS AND ACCESSORIES 22

CHAPTER 2: MATERIALS TO USE WITH CRICUT MACHINE 28

    FABRIC 28

    FOAM 28

    FOIL 29

    PAPER 29

    PLASTIC 30

    VINYL 30

    WOOD 31

    WHAT CAN MY CRICUT DO? 31

CHAPTER 3: CRICUT SOFTWARE 34

    DESIGN SPACE 34

    CRAFT ROOM 34

    MOVING ON TO CREATING YOUR PROJECT TEMPLATE 34

    CRICUT BASIC 36

    SURE CUTS A LOT 37

    CRICUT DESIGNSTUDIO 37

    CRICUT SYNC 37

    PLAY AROUND AND PRACTICE 38

    MAKE THE CUT 38

CHAPTER 4: CRICUT DESIGN 40

WHAT IS THE DESIGN SPACE? 40
WHAT IS THE CRICUT DESIGN CANVAS SPACE AREA? 41
CRICUT DESIGN SPACE CANVAS – WHAT TO DO AND HOW TO DO CANVASSING? 41
CANVAS EDITING AREA 42
TOP EDITING SUBPANEL 43
CANVAS - TOGGLE MENU 43
PROJECT NAME (UNTITLED*) 44
MY PROJECTS 44
SAVE BUTTON 44
MAKER (MACHINE) 45
MAKE IT BUTTON 45
BOTTOM EDITING SUBPANEL 46
UNDO/REDO 46
LINOTYPE 46

CHAPTER 5: SPACE CRICUT PROJECT 50

STARTING A NEW PROJECT - THE BASICS 50
BASIC OBJECT EDITING 53
FUNCTIONS OF THE ALIGNMENT TOOL 54

CHAPTER 6: IDEAS WITH FABRIC 56

TASSELS 57
MONOGRAMMED DRAWSTRING BAG 59
PRINT SOCKS 61
NIGHT SKY PILLOW 63
CLUTCH PURSE 65

CHAPTER 7: IDEAS WITH GLASS 68

    Etched Glass Casserole Dish... 68

    Superhero Beer or Drinking Glasses 71

    Etched Monogrammed Glass 73

    Live, Love, Laugh Glass Block 75

    Unicorn Wine Glass 77

    Window Decoration 80

CHAPTER 8: IDEAS WITH VINYL 82

    Christmas Ornaments 82

    Mason Jar Tags 84

    Cork Coasters 86

    Embellished Shoes 88

    Chipboard puzzle 90

    Shoes Pouch 92

    Sleeping Mask 96

    Vinyl Wall Decals 100

    Vinyl Easter Eggs 102

    Vinyl Sticker Car Window 106

    Bed And Breakfast Guest Room Wood Sign 108

    Wooden Hand-Lettered Sign 111

CHAPTER 9: IDEAS WITH PAPER 114

    Recipe Stickers 114

    Custom Notebooks 117

    Paper Flowers 119

    Crepe Paper Bouquet 121

    Leaf Banner..123

    Paper Pinwheels 125

    Paper Lollipops...127

    Paper Luminary 129

    DIY Paper Marigold Flower 131

    Magnetic Paper Flowers 136

    Paper Succulents in a Container 139

    Creative Herbarium 142

CHAPTER 10: IDEAS WITH CLOTHING 146

    Custom Graphic T-shirt 146

    Halloween T-Shirt 149

    'Queen B' T-shirt 152

    T-Shirts (Vinyl, Iron On) 156

    Matching Family Disney Shirts..160

    Easy Lacey Dress 162

    Dinosaur T-Shirt 164

CONCLUSION 166

Introduction

We should not forget that the cool thing about Cricut is that projects are endless. You might decide to have your own wall lettering, or you might choose to make a nursery at home, and you would need to make that distinct wall painting with several letters. Instead of you to spend several hours cutting with blades and carving with knives or any other cutting device, you just need a Cricut machine. You do not even need to hire a muralist for your hand painting because you can do that yourself. In fact, people like these are happy that you are not exposed to this knowledge so that they can make some cash from you. The die cut machine produces those precise cuts which children and other professional needs. There are several die-cut stickers you can get from this machine. This machine also allows you to render wedding favors and party favors easily by helping in the creating process of tags, bags, boxes, and several other party creations. These pieces can come in several forms like gift bags, banners, hats, etc. These and many more can fit the theme of any party because you are making them. As much as I would love to shy away from the scrapbook stuff, I just cannot. Now, just picture your daughter or your son getting married, and you present him/her with a scrapbook having pictures from the very first day they stepped into this planet to where they are now. Gifts like this sound odd, but they are invaluable because you are not giving out a utensil or a tool, you are giving out those memories. Scrapbooks carry out a lot of memories and those feelings you cannot give through your regular gifts.

If you have a Cricut machine and you have not gotten these supplies, I would advise that you get them as soon as possible. We are aware that these supplies are grouped into different categories. First is the paper category, which includes; adhesive cardstock, cereal box, copy paper, flocked paper, cardboard paper, Notebook paper, flocked cardstock, foil embossed paper, Freezer Paper, Glitter Paper, Kraft paper, Kraft Board, metallic Paper, Metallic Poster board, Photographs, Poster Board, Rice Paper, Solid core Cardstock, Wax Paper, Photo Framing Mat, White Core Cardstock, Photo Framing mat, Watercolor Paper, Freezer Paper, Foil Poster Board, etc.

We should not forget that the Vinyl is another material which you need to make your work on the Cricut machine smooth. The Cricut machine can work on those beautiful materials, which can be used to make decals, stencils, graphics, and those beautiful signs too. You can cut through the following vinyl materials, chalkboard vinyl, dry erase vinyl, holographic vinyl, stencil vinyl, printable vinyl, Matte Vinyl, Adhesive Vinyl, Printable Vinyl, and also Glossy Vinyl. Furthermore, you may have so much experience in the fabric and Textile world, and you want to infuse the Cricut machine. Some of the materials or fabrics that you can work with are; canvas, denim, cotton fabric, linen, leather, flannel, burlap, duck cloth, felt, metallic leather, polyester, printable fabrics, silk, wool felt, and many more others. If you have not got your Iron-on Vinyl. Which is meant to be the heat transfer vinyl. You make use of this vinyl to decorate a T-shirt, tote bags, and other kind of fabric items that you can think of like; Printable Iron On, Glitter Iron-on, Glossy Iron On, Flocked Iron-on, Holographic sparkle iron-on, Metallic Iron-on, Neon Iron-on, Foil Iron-on, etc.

We should not narrow our minds to the materials mentioned above because there are several other materials which the Cricut can cut through or even work on some of them include; adhesive wood, cork board, Balsa Wood, craft foam, aluminum sheets, corrugated paper, Embossable foil, Foil Acetate, Paint Chips, Plastic Packaging, Metallic Vellum, Printable Sticker Paper, Stencil material, Shrink Plastic, Wrapping Paper, Window Cling, Wood Veneer, Washi Tape, Birch Wood, Wrapping Paper, Wood Veneer, Plastic Packaging, Soda Can, Glitter Foam, Printable Magnet Sheets, etc. The Cricut maker can work on materials that are up to 2.4mm thick and other special materials and special fabrics like; Jersey, Cashmere, Chiffon, Terry Cloth, Tweed, Velvet, Jute, Knits, Moleskin, Fleece, and several others.

This machine can be found anywhere and everywhere, so much paper artwork is done. What this suggests is that you can see these machines in schools, offices, craft shops, etc. you can make use of this Cricut machine for a school project, card stock projects as well as iron-on projects too. Making use of this machine to cut out window clings is not a bad idea at all. It is not limited to this because you also engage in projects that have to do with adhesive stencil and stencil vinyl also. You would remove the stencil vinyl after it is dried. This would leave a distinct imprint. You can also make use of this machine to create lovely fashion accessories like several pieces of jewelry. The Cricut machine allows you to make use of the faux leather for exceptional designs. Recall that we talked about school projects. Preschoolers and their instructors can benefit from this machine. Furthermore, you can print out photos or images from your computer while making use of this machine, especially from the printable magnets to those sticker papers, customized gifts, bags, etc.

Defining objects requires you to use other similar objects to drive home your point and to give the reader a clearer picture. The very available way we can describe a Cricut machine is to say that it is a machine that has so much resemblance with the printer, but it is used majorly for cutting designed pieces. That is a very simple and easy definition, you do not need to bother yourself about that. Just picture a printer in your mind and think of a cutting device. Oh, no, you already have the Cricut machine with you, right? You would notice that it uses precise blades and several templates or rollers during cutting.

Against what people think. The machine is not meant for scrapbook keepers or makers alone. I still do not know why this idea has become so much rooted in the minds of people that we have grown to allow this thought to dominate our reactions and attitude towards any new innovation.

The world has been transformed with that machine, as its products have been able to add those special visual beauties to the simple paperwork that we know. The Cricut machine has several models and versions, some of them include Cricut Expression, Expression 2, Cricut Imagine, Cricut Gypsy, Cricut Cake Mini, Cricut Personal Cutter, Cricut Crafts Edition, and Martha Stewart and the Cricut Explore Air. The tool obviously fits into any type of craft you are working on. And there is also a die cut machine which gives you that extra-precise, sharp, and smart cutting. The process of cutting materials by hand during crafts has been reduced drastically, thanks to this wonderful machine. More also, you can perform multiple projects all at the same time due to the effectiveness of this device. It contains several cartridges, which are always available to help you explore different forms and shapes of several designs. More also that move from one project to another has been made possible with the use of this Cricut machine. Any material can be shaped into that design you want it to be. Furthermore, you can also create patterns that are already pre-installed in the software that comes with it. The design software tool becomes very much available with pre-loaded designs for instant use. I am sure you must have been able to purchase this machine from your local craft store on the online store. You are aware that the price was based on the kind of model you are using and I am sure that you've been able to narrow down your needs for you to be able to get your machine because anything which makes your work easier and faster is a very important investment and the Cricut machine is definitely one. Due to the efficiency of this machine, we now have it in several places we never thought it would be in years. We have them in offices and specific workshops. If you think that the Cricut is a home-only tool, you are quite wrong. This time-saving device allows your work to be very professional, and the beautiful thing about it is that we have no limits to what it can do. I am sure that you are reading this to gain more ideas and you hastily want to jump into making things and doing some stuff. Yes, that is cool; however, we need to understand some basics, otherwise, we would be making serious mistakes, or the process would look very confusing.

CHAPTER 1:

Components of the Cricut

A Cricut is a cutting machine that lets you cut and create beautiful, magnificent crafts with materials that you didn't even know existed. You can also sketch, emboss, and create folding lines to realize 3D designs, greeting cards, bags, and a lot more, which is based on the layout that you may have.

Cricut allowed crafting and cutting difficult designs skillfully and in a presentable manner. It all started with the invention of the Cricut machine. It works like a printer but has better features that can be used in every field to beautify it.

You create a sketch and submit the design to the Cricut on your device or phone. The Cricut works like a printer and takes the template out of the item you bring inside. The most significant difference between a printer and the Cricut is that a Cricut print out the image from an entity so that the image is duplicated on paper. The Cricut features a dial on it with a variety of materials labeled on it, which you can use as your design piece. What makes the Cricut unique is that it can be used much like a printer too. You will tell the computer to draw the template on paper by placing a marker thereon. Looking at the design, to designers and artisans, this seems like paradise. The Cricut computer also has the tools that you can use for a cartridge library. Just check for the form you like in the library and give the order to the printer to print it out, and you are ready to go. The blade set up in the Cricut is a sharp one that performs its functions exceptionally cleanly. For each corner, the cutouts are immaculate, and each edge is cut out precisely, as seen on the screen.

The Cricut machine is a machine type of Machine without limits. Your ingenuity, the vision, is beyond limits. It is not only limited to designers and artisans. The function of this computer is such that you can use it to simply mold anything you want if you know how to do it. So, you do not need to stay away from it simply because you are not an artist. Embrace the imagination inside and build whatever you want. The Cricut is a perfect tool for people who enjoy craftsmanship and for people who need to cut multiple items and all kinds of material.

The good thing about Cricut is that there are wide varieties of cartridges available in the market to meet the demands of any occasion. How you use your Cricut machines to decorate your home with angel shaped cutouts or pine shapes this Christmas, you'll find Cricut Christmas cartridges easily available. From reindeer to an army of snowmen, from Christmas trees to villages, you can have them all with special Cricut Christmas cartridges. Want to make decorative cards for your family friends this Christmas, let the Cricut cartridge do that for you. If the birthday of a loved one is coming, there are lots of designs to choose from. Or you want to host a themed New Year party with unique decorations of various patterns to match your theme, and you'll be amazed at the wide variety of Cricut cartridges you can find in the market. All of these are possible with the amazing Cricut machine.

The Cricut machine is Robert Workman's innovation that partnered with fellow inventors Jonathan Johnson, Matt Strong, and Phil Jeffrey to create a technology that has generated millions in sales revenue in just a few years.

For decades, Robert's company Provo Craft has been selling art goods to customers, who claimed that a mechanical tool for cutting material forms would be a solution to hand cutting materials issues. The design industry has an annual revenue of $30 billion and a four-year cumulative growth trend of 2.6 percent, according to the Association of Crafts and Creative Industries. Fifty-seven percent of American households spend an average of $476 each year on crafts. While school projects account for a substantial share of the craft market, scrapbooking is the top-selling craft that has doubled in size over the last few years. Creating Keepsakes Magazine says this sport has exceeded golf in popularity in the United States. One out of four households has a resident interested in scrapbooking, like one out of five families that have someone playing golf.

Robert offers inventors some positive advice. He advises that consumers should canvass and listen, "Don't do it without their feedback." He proposes that inventors should be frank about their abilities and shortcomings and that they should set up a team to produce and sell their ideas. "You can log everything you do and deeply analyze the business and competition. Because of its precision, efficiency, longevity, and functionality, the Cricut speech system and Cricut cartridges dominate the electronic cutter sector.

Models Overview

Cricut Explore One

Explore One is ideal for beginners and inexperienced users who want to get into die-cutting, craft cutting, and plotting. The machine is not advanced like the other Explore models, and it is also the cheapest Cricut machine you can get.

Capability:

The machine is also highly capable, even if it's an old model. The system can also handle scoring and writing smoothly.

Materials:

Regardless of the simplicity and the inexpensive nature of the machine, it is still highly capable.

Cricut Explore Air

While this is quite similar to the Explore One model, it also comes with some additional features.

The main difference between them is the presence of the inbuilt Bluetooth adapter. If you don't enjoy seeing cables and wires all around your workplace, especially with the danger of tripping over them, then this model solves that problem.

Capability

The Explore Air is also different from Explore One because it features a double carriage. It means that you can draw, write, or score while you cut because it has two clamps to hold both tools. It saves you money because you don't have to purchase a tool adapter.

Cutting Force

The system is more powerful than the older model when it comes to the cutting force. It features a Cut Smart technology made by Cricut, which enhances the blade control of the system and gives your creations a more professional look. It can cut anything that is as wide as 23.5 inches accurately and precisely.

It also has the Smart Set dial, which increases the control you have over your project's cutting.

The features of the Cricut Design Space are very similar. But, when using Explore Air, you get more freedom, and you are allowed to use .svg, .gif, and .dxf files in addition to the standard files allowed with Explore One.

Sadly, Explore Air does not have either a knife or a rotary blade. Because of these two types of blades, the Explore Air recommends for more light crafts and scrapbooking. It does have an inbuilt cutter, though.

A brand new Explore Airbox comes with these tools:

- A 25.4 x 10 x 9.2 inches Cricut Explore Sir machine with inbuilt Bluetooth technology
- It has an inbuilt accessory adapter.
- Inbuilt blade.
- USB and power cord.
- Metallic silver marker.
- Iron-on sample.
- Cardstock sample.
- Over 100 images,
- Over 50 ready-to-cut projects.
- 12" x 12" Standard Grip cutting mat.
- Welcome guide.

Cricut Explore Air 2

It is the youngest sibling of the Cricut Explore line. It is the best of the machines in this line. Explore Air 2 as efficiently as the other ones, but it does its work even better. It even has a better design, and it comes in different colors.

Cricut Maker

The newest Cricut die-cutting machine is the Cricut Maker. If you thought that the Explore Air 2 was a great model, then you should get ready to be blown away.

The Cricut Maker is a rare unit amongst other die-cutting machines. The rotary blade is already enough to attract experienced users. For beginners, it provides an avenue for improvement and unlimited creativity.

The Cricut Maker, as an updated version of others, is mighty and flexible. It comes with a toolkit that includes a rotary blade, knife blade, deep cut blade, and fine point blade. It also comes with a single and a double scoring wheel and a collection of pens. The pens include a fine point pen, a washable fabric pen, a calligraphy pen, and a scoring stylus.

The machine also improves its efficiency by adding some unique features. We have the adaptive tool system, which means that the device can automatically adjust the blade's angle and the edge's pressure depending on the material. It doesn't need the Smart dial feature because the Cricut Maker determines your cutting force for you, and its decisions are usually accurate.

It has two clamps, one for the pen or scoring tool and the other for the cutting blade. This system is also unique because of its fast mode and precise mode. It works for any paper, cardstock, and vinyl.

Materials

As expected, the Cricut Maker will handle more and thicker materials than the Cricut Explore series machines.

From light materials to basswood and leather, this machine will exceed your expectations.

Cricut Design Space also provides a lot of benefits for Cricut Maker users/. It allows .jpg, .gif, .png,.svg, .bmp and .dxf files.

The system also supports a wireless Bluetooth adapter. You can also enjoy the Sewing Pattern Library if you own a Cricut Maker. The library contains 50 ready-to-cut projects, and it is a result of a partnership between Cricut and Riley Blake Designs.

Another great benefit you get when using Cricut Maker with Design Space is to get Cricut Access free membership for a trial period.

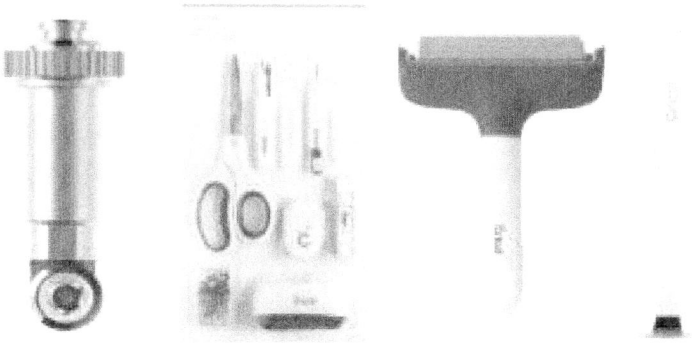

The only downsides to this model are that it is relatively slow when working with very thick materials, although that expects. It also produces a lot of noise because of the fast mode.

It is what comes in the new Cricut Maker box.

Which Cricut Model Should You Use?

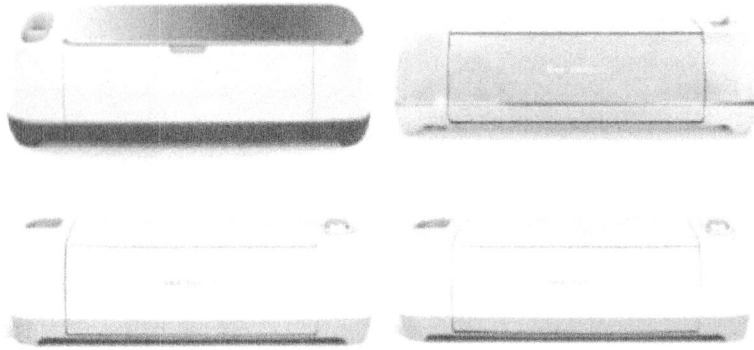

Although all Cricut models are great, the Cricut Maker or Explore Air models highly recommend, whether you're a beginner or an advanced user. These two machines are usually ideal for most people, no matter the type of craft you use.

For the person looking to go into serious crafting, woodworking, sewing, and quilting, then the Cricut Maker is highly recommended. It is highly professional, and it can work for any craft that you get. The system has a lot of benefits, especially in Design Space.

If you are a beginner who wants to start handmade, you should also buy Cricut Maker, because it doesn't make sense to buy an old model and accumulate experience before purchasing a new model.

You might be planning on using your Cricut machine for business purposes. It will mean that you will be repeating the same action occasionally.

For this use, you can use the Cricut Explore Air 2 because it has a fast mode and many other advantages.

Beginners, leisurely crafters, and those who have a tight budget will work better with the Cricut Explore One and Explore Air.

Tools and Accessories

Cricut has much to offer in the way of tools and accessories. There are machines they offer to suit different crafting purposes, which have their own accessories and tools as well.

For the Cricut cutting machines, here is what's available:

Cricut Maker Cutting Blades

In addition to the Explore Cutting blade, the Cricut Maker has additional cutting blades that allow for intricate cutting details on a variety of materials.

The Cricut Maker comes with one additional blade, the revolutionary rotary cutting blade for use on cutting all sorts of fabrics. Unlike the average rotary blade, this one lasts far longer because it avoids the nicks that typically come with its line of duty. You can buy additional blades individually, but one blade should last throughout multiple projects.

Cutting Mats

Cricut cutting mats come in a variety of sizes and degrees of stickiness. Depending on what material you are using, you will want less or more stickiness on your mat to hold the material in place while cutting.

The Circuit Weeder

The weeder tool, which looks similar to a dental pick, is used for removing negative space from a vinyl project. This weeder tool is a must when doing any type of project that involves vinyl. Trying to get rid of access vinyl is nearly impossible without a weeder, especially with materials like glitter iron-on. A weeder is a useful tool for any type of project using adhesives. Instead of picking up the adhesive with your fingertips, use the weeder tool, and keep your fingers sticky mess free!

The Cricut Scraper

The Circuit Scraper tool is essential (and a lifesaver!) when you need to rid your cutting mat of excess negative bits. This tool typically works best with paper, such as cardstock, but other materials can easily be scraped up as well. Use the flexibility of the mat to your advantage as you scrap the bits off the mat to ensure you are not scraping up the adhesive on the mat as well. You can also use the Cricut Scraper as a score line holder, which allows you to fold over the score-line with a nice crisp edge. It can also be used as a burnishing tool for Cricut transfer tape, as it will allow seamless separation of the transfer tape from the backing.

The Cricut Spatula

A spatula is a must-have tool for a crafter who works with a lot of paper. Pulling the paper off of a Cricut cut mat can result in a lot of tearing and paper curling if you are not diligent and mindful when you are removing it. The spatula is thinly designed to slip right under paper, which allows you to ease it off the mat carefully. Be sure to clean it often, as it is likely to get the adhesive build up on it after multiple uses. It can also be used as a scraper if your scraper tool is not readily available!

Scissors

These sharp tools come in handy more often than you can possibly know with Cricut projects, and having a dedicated pair makes it so much easier to complete your projects.

Craft Tweezers

These reverse-action tweezers have a strong grip, precise points, and alleviate cramping after prolonged use.

Spatula

Sometimes you feel like you need an extra set of hands when you're peeling or laying down a project

. This tool gives you that extra support and maneuverability where you need it.

Scoring Stylus

This tool can be loaded into clamp A in your Cricut machine. This will allow the machine to draw deep lines into your project to give it texture or a precise folding point.

This same effect can be achieved with other tools on the market, but Cricut makes it simpler and faster with this accessory.

Portable Trimmer

This is a precision cutting tool that allows you to get fast, crisp, straight cuts on your projects 100% of the time.

Other versions of this product are available on the market, so keep your eye out for ones with great reviews and a low price point.

Rotary Cutting Kit

This kit includes a gridded cutting mat and a rotary cutting tool. Cuts are fast, sharp, and precise. This is far from the only rotary tool available on the market, and it's great for cutting fabric and scrapbook pieces.

XL Scraper/Burnishing Tool

This provides a level of control that cannot be beaten. It exerts pressure evenly and helps to eliminate uneven layering and air bubbles. This tool comes very highly recommended by the community of users.

Paper Crafting Set – If you're particularly into papercraft, you will find the edge distresser, quilling tool, piercing tool, and craft mat in this set to be quite to your liking. Quilling or paper filigree art is gaining popularity these days, and these are some of the best tools available for that craft.

TrueControl™ Knife

This is a precision blade that is comparable to XACTO in quality and in type. For more precise freehand cuts, this knife is very helpful at any crafting station.

Cricut Explore® Wireless Bluetooth® Adapter

This product is to help your Cricut Explore machine connect with Bluetooth to your computer or device. The Cricut Maker has this capability built-in, but it can be added to your Explore machine as well.

Deep-Point Replacement Blades

These help your Cricut machine to make more precise cuts with thicker materials!

Bonded Fabric Blades

These blades are meant to retain their extremely sharp point, cut after cut into fabric in your machine!

Replacement Blades

With different purposes like debossing, engraving, perforation, and more, it can be purchased from Cricut as well.

These are specifically for the Cricut Maker model, whereas the replacement blades specified above are for the Cricut Explore models.

The Cricut Easy Press

If you begin to venture into iron-on projects and want to upgrade from a traditional iron and ironing board, the Cricut Easy press is the right way to go. It will make projects so much easier than using a traditional iron. The Cricut Easy Press is known to help keep designed adhered for longer, essentially no more peeling of designs after one or two uses and washes. The Easy press also takes all of the guesswork out of the right amount of contact time as well as temperature. You will not run the risk of burning your transfer paper or fabric!

The Cricut Brightpad

The lightweight and low profile design of the Cricut Brightpad reduces eyestrain while making crafting easier. It is designed to illuminate fine lines for tracing, cut lines for weeding, and so much more! It is thin and lightweight, which allows for durable transportation. BrightPad makes crafting more enjoyable with its adjustable, evenly lit surface. The bright LED lights can be adjusted depending on the workspace. The only downfall to this accessory is that it must be plugged in while it is used. It does not contain a rechargeable battery.

The Cricut Cuttlebug Machine

The Cricut Cuttlebug is an embossing and dies cutting machine that offers portability and versatility when it comes to cutting and embossing a wide variety of materials. This machine gives professional looking results with clean, crisp, and deep embosses. This machine goes beyond paper, allowing you to emboss tissue paper, foils, thin leather, and more!

CHAPTER 2:

Materials to Use with Cricut Machine

Cricut boasts being able to work with more than 100 materials to make your projects come to life like never before. Thanks to the vast assortment of media that Cricut can bring to your crafting station, the sky is the limit for what you can do with your Cricut machine, no matter which model you've elected to purchase.

Here are the materials that your Cricut can use without issue!

Fabric

- Polyester
- Linen
- Printable Fabric
- Silk
- Cotton Fabric
- Wool Felt
- Canvas
- Metallic Leather
- Oil Cloth
- Felt
- Faux Suede
- Flannel
- Denim
- Burlap
- Duck Cloth
- Leather
- Faux Leather

Foam

- Glitter Foam
- Craft Foam

Foil

- Aluminum Foil
- Embossable Foil
- Aluminum Sheets
- Foil Poster Board
- Foil Embossed Paper
- Adhesive Foil
- Foil Iron-On
- Foil Acetate

Paper

- Poster Board
- Contact Paper
- Metallic Paper
- Glitter Cardstock
- Solid Core Cardstock
- Flocked Cardstock
- Printable Sticker Paper
- Notebook Paper
- Parchment Paper
- Photo Framing Mat
- Metallic Vellum
- Vellum
- Freezer Paper
- Metallic Cardstock
- Flocked Paper
- Metallic Poster Board
- Corrugated Paper
- Peal Cardstock
- Glitter Paper
- Paper Board
- Tissue Paper
- Rice Paper
- Cardboard
- Shimmer Paper
- Pearl Paper
- Craft Paper

- Photographs
- Cardstock
- Temporary Tattoo Paper
- Copy Paper
- Washi Sheets
- Scrapbook Paper
- Post Its
- Construction Paper
- Washi Tape
- Paper Grocery Bags
- Adhesive Cardstock
- Wrapping Paper

Plastic

- Shrink Plastic
- Transparency Film
- Duct Tape
- Window Cling
- Magnet Sheets
- Plastic Packaging
- Stencil Material
- Printable Magnet Sheets

Vinyl

- Holographic Iron-On
- Removable Adhesive Vinyl
- Flocked Iron-On
- Neon Iron-On
- Matte Vinyl
- Metallic Vinyl
- Stencil Vinyl
- Outdoor Vinyl
- Adhesive Vinyl
- Printable Vinyl
- Printable Iron-On
- Glitter Vinyl
- Glossy Vinyl
- Glossy Iron-On

- Chalkboard Vinyl
- Matte Iron-On
- Glitter Iron-On
- Permanent Adhesive Vinyl
- Dry Erase Vinyl
- Holographic Vinyl
- Metallic Iron-On
- Paint Chips

Wood

- Chipboard
- Wood Veneer
- Adhesive Wood
- Corkboard
- Balsa Wood
- Birch Wood

What Can My Cricut Do?

There really isn't any limit to how much you can do with your Cricut machine. However, if you're short on ideas, here are some that I've thrown together to get your creative juices flowing!

Take a look through this list and come up with some things that you think would fit well with the types of designs that you like to make!

- Make felt dolls
- Beautifully address envelopes
- Create doll clothing
- Make greeting cards of every design and style
- Create placards
- Cut items out of balsa wood

- Cut washi tape shapes
- Craft borders and decorations for your corkboard
- Dream up refrigerator magnets
- Customize wedding invitations
- Create holiday crafts
- Design or decorate purses and wallets
- Cut your own craft foam shapes
- Create decals and patterns for pillows and cushions
- Create your own coloring book pages
- Cut fabric with precision
- Make jewelry
- Make party favors
- Create 3D bouquets
- Cut leather
- Cut your own party hats
- Make themed window clings
- Create fabric appliques
- Create temporary tattoos

- Create glassware decals
- Design personalized gift tags
- Create clothes for your pet
- Create custom gift boxes
- Customize baby clothes
- Design creative pin cushions
- Create cake toppers
- Customize holiday ornaments
- Custom Coasters
- Create sewing patterns
- Create themed t-shirt transfers
- Make personalized fabric key fobs
- Cut perfect quilting squares

CHAPTER 3:

Cricut Software

Design Space

Design Space is for any Explore machine with a high-speed, broadband Internet connection that is connected to a computer or an iOS device. This more advanced software allows full creative control for users with Cricut machines.

Craft Room

Some machines, such as the Explore and Explore Air, cannot use Craft Room, but many other models can.

Craft Room users also have access to a free digital cartridge, which offers images that all Cricut machines can cut.

Moving on to Creating Your Project Template

On the home page, select "New Project," which will be followed by a page with a blank canvas that looks like the grid on your Cricut mats. To any artist, the words "empty canvas" is a nightmare in itself, so please just bear with me since we will fill that bad boy up in a second. But first, let's go through the menu options.

New Templates, Projects, Images, Text, Shapes, and Upload. These are the things that you will see on your left-hand side when you have the canvas open on the screen.

New

New means that you will start a new project and clicking the tab will redirect you to a blank canvas. Be sure to save all changes on your current project before you go to the new canvas. Otherwise, you will lose all of the progress you have already made on that design.

Templates

Clicking on Templates will allow you to set a template to help you visualize and work with sizing. It is very handy for someone who is not familiar with Cricut Design Space and doesn't know what sizes to set. If you are cutting out wearable items on fabric, you can change the size of the template to fit whoever will be wearing it. I'm sure you can agree that this feature is especially beneficial for the seamstresses out there.

Projects

Projects, meanwhile, will lead you to the ready-to-make projects so that you can start cutting right away. Some of the projects are not customizable, but others are when you open the template, which is pretty cool.

Many of these are not free either, which irks me to a new extent. You can choose the "Free for Cricut (whatever machine you have)," and the projects that will turn up won't have to be paid for.

Images

Images are where you can search for thousands of photos to use for the craft.

Those images with the green flag with the "A" on them are the ones that come only with Cricut Access, so be aware if you do not have it. It is sort of like a Pinterest image search engine with a lot of pictures in its database.

Text

The Text basically goes without saying. When you select this option, you can type whatever you want and scale it onto your canvas. You may select any font saved on your computer; that's why collecting those has never been more useful! There is also an option called "multi-layered font," which gives your text a shadow layer. If you are cutting out the letters and shadow layers, the Cricut will do them separately and combine the two later if you wish to. It can create very cool effects, so make sure you try that option out. Furthermore, remember that when you are being paid to do a job, the font you are using might require a license to use.

Shapes

Shapes allow you add basic forms to your canvas, which you can tweak to fit your own needs. The shapes include circle, square, rectangle, triangle, et cetera.

Upload

When you click the Upload tab, you can upload your own images and transform them into cuttable pieces. This, along with the text, is the only reason why I still use Design Space. It is really awesome to be able to use this feature.

Cricut Basic

This is a program or software designed to help the new user get an easy start on designing new crafts and DIY projects. This system will help you with image selection to cutting with the least amount of time spent in the design stages.

You can locate your image, pre-set projector font, and immediately print, cut, score, and align with tools that are found within the program. You can use this program on the iOS 7.1.2 or later systems as well as iPad and several of the iPhones from the Mini to the 5th generation iPod touch. Since it is also a cloud-based service, you are able to start on one device and finish from another.

Sure Cuts a Lot

This is another third-party software that has a funny name that gives you the ability to take control of your designs without some of the limitations that can happen when using cartridges used within the Cricut DesignStudio. You will need to install an update to your software to use this program; you can download it for free. It allows for the use of TrueType and OpenType font formats as well as simple drawing and editing tools. You can import any file format and then convert it to the one that you need. There is an option for blackout and shadow.

Cricut DesignStudio

This program allows you to connect with your software and provides you with much more functionality as far as shapes and fonts are concerned. There are various options for tools that provide you resources for designing more creative images. You will be able to flip, rotate, weld, or slant the images and fonts. However, you will still be limited in the amounts or types of fonts that you can use based on the ones on the cartridges. There is a higher level of software features that allow for customization.

Cricut Sync

This is a program designed for updating the Cricut Expression 2 as well as the Imagine machine and the Gypsy device. You just connect your system to the computer and run the synced program for an installation of updates on the features that come with your machine.

This is also used to troubleshoot many issues that could arise from the hardware.

Play Around and Practice

You can combine your shapes and images, add some text, and create patterns. The possibilities are endless. The best thing to do is familiarize yourself with the software before you attempt to cut expensive materials. Start small and cheap - printer paper will be an ideal choice - and cut away. See what works well for you and stick with it. There are many options concerning the Cricut Design Space, and the only way to learn all of this is to experiment and click on every tab you see and try different combinations of options when playing around on the software.

Make the Cut

This is a third-party program that works with the Cricut design software. It offers a straightforward look at the design features that Cricut has. This system can convert a raster image into a vector so that you can cut it. There is also a great way to do lattice tools. It uses many file formats and TrueType fonts. There are advanced tools for editing and an interface that is easy to learn and use. This system works with Craft ROBO, Gazelle, Silhouette, Wishblade, and others. It allows you to import any file from a TTF, OTF, PDF, GSD, and so on and convert them to JPG, SVG, PDF, and so on. It is flexible and user-friendly.

CHAPTER 4:

Cricut Design

Now that you are familiar with all the Cricut machine models you can use for your crafting, as well as all the tools, blades, and accessories you can use for your projects, you need to learn more about Design Space before you start with your first Cricut projects for beginners. Before we dive into the magnificent world of Cricut designs and crafting projects made with Cricut, we need to address the very core of designing projects – Cricut machine software known as Design Space. Here is everything you need to know about Design Space before you can start using Cricut for your projects.

What is the Design Space?

Cricut Design Space is a special software created for crafting with Cricut machines, and it represents an open-source software where you can create your designs or use Cricut designs that can be unlocked for access via Design Space. Everything you need for your crafting with the Cricut machine is available with Design Space features and commands. This software will be the starting point of your projects, and this is also where all the magic happens. Design Space is completely free to use, and it comes with purchasing a Cricut machine. There are already ready-to-make designs available in the software while you can access Design Space via multiple devices, including your laptop and your Smartphone. Once you get familiar with all commands you can use with your designs as you are starting from scratch on your projects, you will soon learn that Cricut and Design Space have everything a crafter needs for a project well done. The software needs to be set up when using it for the first time, however, the process is made easy with step-by-step guidance. Once you set up your Design Space, you are ready to go and try out commands and functions the software has to offer. At first, you may find it a bit difficult to get around all the functions and commands, however, we are making sure that you can get familiar with all crucial operations on Design Software, section by section and step by step.

What is the Cricut Design Canvas Space Area?

Canvas Space Area is the part of the software where all the magic of creating projects for Cricut begins. Here is where you will be able to make edits and design your projects before you start cutting towards making your final product. Once you set up your Design Space software, in case you wish to gain access to the library of designs you will need to subscribe to Cricut Access, which provides you with exclusive and premium fonts and designs. You can always make your designs and patterns once you get familiar with the software. When you start working on Design Space, all your designs and edits will be done in the Canvas window. Canvas has multiple icons and commands, which is why we will go through each of the available buttons. By getting familiar with commands, you will soon be able to make your designs and start working on your projects.

Canvas is comprised out of four basic sections, editing area, layers panels, canvas area, and insert area. In this guide, you will find all the needed information on each section of Cricut Design Space Canvas, including the purpose of each section and what needs to be done before you can say that your design is ready for cutting.

Cricut Design Space Canvas – What to Do and How to Do Canvassing?

We will get into the details on how to work in Canvas and how to insert your images and patterns, edit your designs, and perform other actions that can be done in Design Space.

Let's see how you can start working in Canvas, step-by-step.

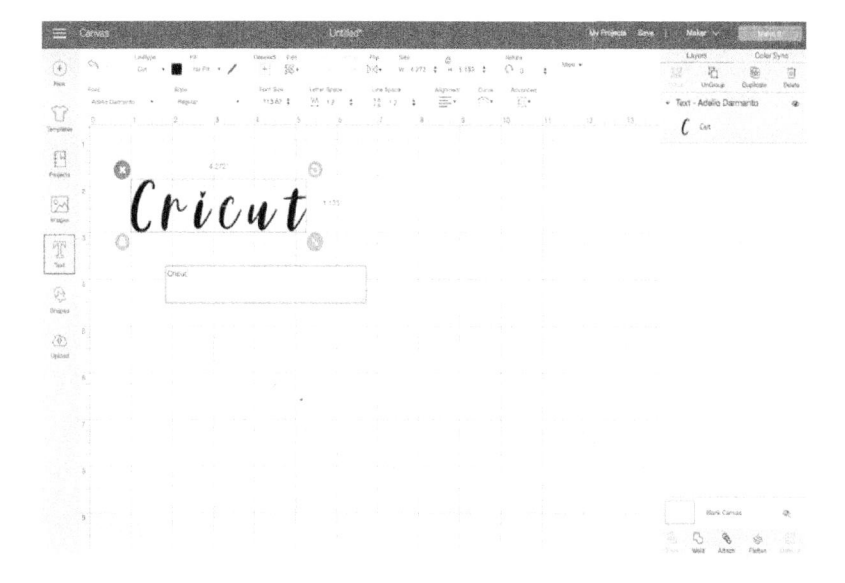

This is how the Canvas window looks like when active, while you can also notice that you have numerous options and commands within the software.

Canvas Editing Area

The canvas editing area is the section where you will do all your edits, which includes arranging project elements in the canvas area and editing your designs. The editing area is located on the top of the Canvas and also allows changing fonts, size of fonts and designs as well as enables alignment of design pieces. This is where you are preparing your project from scratch. The editing area/panel can be divided into two sub-areas or subpanels. The top panel of the Canvas editing area serves the purpose of holding the main functions for creating new projects, save your projects once your design is ready and send your designs to the machine to start making projects. The second sub-panel found at the bottom of the Canvas editing panel holds commands for designing and editing your projects.

Top Editing Subpanel

The top editing subpanel comprises several important functions. If you click on "Canvas," you will gain access to the Toggle menu – more details on what you can do with the Toggle menu will be disclosed further. You can also see the next command shown as "Untitled" – This is where you name your projects, following the list of your saved projects under "My project," "Save" button, and "Maker" (Machine button) and the execution button "Make it" colored in green.

Canvas - Toggle Menu

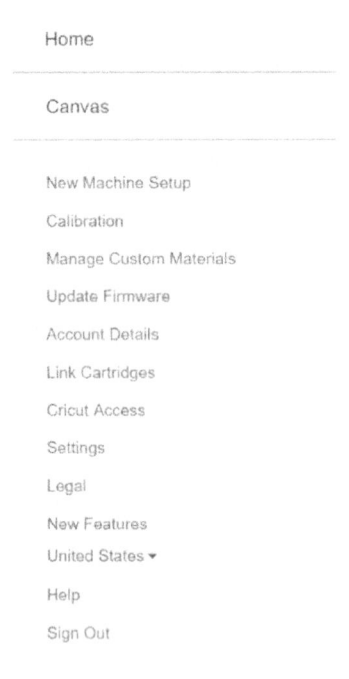

Although you can gain access to the Toggle menu through the "Canvas" menu and Canvas window, the Toggle menu is not directly related to editing functions and commands crucial for working in the editing area of Canvas. Still, it would be handy for you to find your way around the

Toggle menu, which is why we are also addressing these commands as well. You will find all commands regarding the software right here in this dropping menu. You can view your profile from the Toggle menu, update your firmware and software, perform setup for your new machine, check your account details, link cartridges, manage your subscription through Cricut Access, access settings, features and find the Help button for support from Cricut. You can also sign out from your account through the Toggle menu. The settings option will allow adjusting the visibility and measurements for your Canvas area.

Project Name (Untitled*)

All new projects start with "Untitled" tags, while this is the area where you can name your projects that can be later viewed and accessed under the "My projects" section. You won't be able to name your project until you start working in the sense of adding at least one element to the Canvas area.

My Projects

Every project you save and name can be found under "My projects," you can save as many projects as you like and reuse them by redesigning, re-cutting, and editing. This is where you will find an entire list of all the saved projects, which is handy since you might want to work on a project similar to what you have already done. That way you don't always need to start from scratch.

Save Button

Save option won't be available until you start working in the Canvas area and have at least placed one element or pattern on the Canvas. Once you start working, the Save button will become active, and you can click on it to save your projects. All projects are saved on the Cricut cloud storage space, while you can also save your project as you are working on it to prevent losing your work in case of a potential crash of the cloud system. This is less likely to happen, but if you want to be on the safe side, you can save your project as you are working on it, saving your project every time you make some progress.

Maker (Machine)

You can click on this button to access your machine options. This button represents your Cricut machine, and depending on which machine you have and use for crafting, you will have different options available.

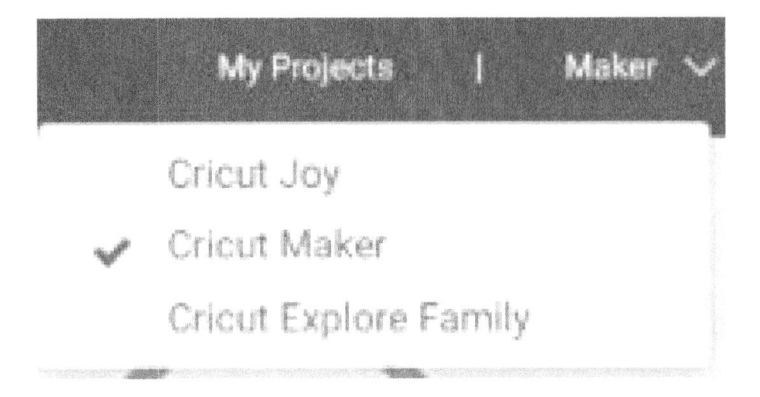

Once you click on the Maker option (machine), you will access all your machines that have been already set up in case you are using more than one Cricut model. Model Maker has different options than other machines

Make It Button

Once you have finished with editing and designing, you can save your project in case you wish to keep it in the My Projects library, then click on the Make it button to prepare for cutting. You can prepare several mats at the time, preparing more cuts and placing them in the queue. You can choose which design should be cut first as you will have all your prepared mats categorized by color on the left side of the window.

Bottom Editing Subpanel

The second subpanel of the editing menu has multiple controls for designing and editing your projects. In case you have already worked with software such as Illustrator, Photoshop, or similar software, you will find most commands familiar. Even if you have never worked on similar software, you will find most of the commands and options to be logical and self-explanatory.

Nevertheless, to help you find your way around the editing panel, we will go through each command available in the second subpanel. You will use these functions to edit your materials and create your designs.

Undo/Redo

This is probably a familiar function, as you can use these buttons (arrows) to correct your mistakes and get back to the previous version of your design in a click. Making mistakes and changing your mind on shapes and colors is a natural thing when during the creative process, which is how these buttons become more than handy.

Linotype

Linotype and fill are options related to the type of blade you wish to use on a given project. Depending on which Cricut machine model you are using, you will have different options for cutting. Once you choose the machine you want to cut with, you will be presented with different types of blades and cutting available for that machine. Based on which material you are using for your project you can choose the type of blade. As far as options for cutting style concerned, you have more than several options to choose from – Wave, Perforation, Deboss, Score, Engrave, Cut, and Draw. All of these options are available with Cricut Maker. In case you are using other machines, there will be fewer options to choose from, making the cutting styles more basic when compared to options available with Maker.

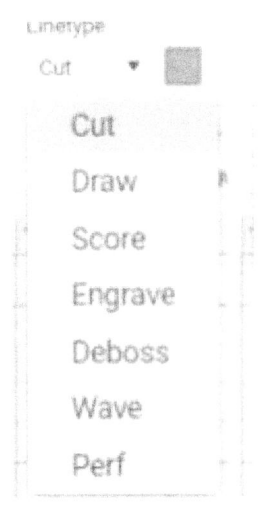

This is how the dropdown menu will look like if you are using Maker once you click on the Linotype option. As you may notice, in case you are using Explore instead of Maker, there will be only three options to choose from.

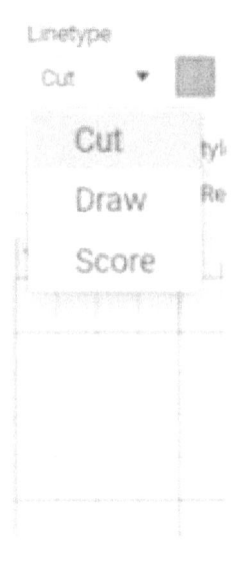

The "Cut" option will be your default line type until you have uploaded your design file, which is when you can choose other options as well. The machine won't cut your design until you choose the "Make it" command.

CHAPTER 5:

Space Cricut Project

Now, you're ready to design your first project, but where do you begin?

At the beginning, of course! Let me walk you through it.

Starting a New Project - The Basics

When starting a new project, you'll want to know what that project will be and what materials you will be using before doing anything else.

For example, if you want to cut vinyl letters to place on wood, you'll need to know all of your dimensions, so your letters fit evenly and centered on the wood. You'll need wood that vinyl can adhere to without the risk of peeling. And you'll want to make certain that your wood is sanded and finished to your desire because you don't want any imperfections. You may find even with store-bought wood pieces advertised as ready-to-use, there are tiny imperfections.

You want to make sure when working with fabric that you know what inks or vinyls will adhere to the surface. You don't want any peeling or cracking to happen to your beautiful design.

When working with any kind of fabric, including canvas bags, you'll want to prewash for sizing because shrinkage, after your design has been set, can cause the design to become distorted.

If you aren't sure exactly what you want to do, have something in mind so that you aren't wasting a lot of materials by trial and error. The cost of crafting materials can add up, so you'll want to eliminate as much potential waste as possible.

If you're new to Cricut Design Space, start with something simple. You don't want to get in over your head. That's the worst thing you can do when you learn any new craft. There are many used Cricut machines for sale, and while some users sell because they upgraded, others are users who gave up. You made the investment, and you'll want to get a return on that investment.

Ready to conquer Cricut Design Space?

To keep up with any changes, you should subscribe to the company email list or check the Cricut website often.

Let's begin by clicking on "New" from our menu options. It's at the very top of the canvas in the left corner.

An empty canvas will appear. You might have previously started a project, and in that case, the machine will detect it in the queue, and you'll be asked if you want to replace the project. If you don't want to replace it, be sure you save all of your changes, or you might lose them, and you don't want to lose all of your hard work. It's important not to rush so that you don't accidentally delete a project you want to be saved. When you've completed that action, you'll be returned to your new blank canvas.

First, you want to name your project. Use a name that closely relates to it, so you aren't getting projects confused. If you have a lot of projects, and you don't use a system to identify them, you might want to consider it.

As you can see from our illustration, everything you need is on the left, under the "new" icon.

Different templates by clicking on the templates icon, however, these are only for viewing to get an idea of how your final project will look.

Projects allow you to access the Make It Now™ platform. There are so many to choose from, and you might find yourself spending a lot of time looking at them all.

Images are just what it says. This is the icon you need to add an image or images to your project.

Text is for writing the text if your project has words.

Shapes allow you to add different shapes such as circles, squares, and hearts.

Upload your images and begin cutting. This is the final design step!

If you know what your project is going to be, you can go to the "projects" icon and begin to customize it or start cutting.

We have talked about subscriptions, and it should be noted that you can purchase a one-time design for a nominal fee. You can also purchase designs from Etsy and other craft sites.

When you've done your design, don't forget to save it. You will get the option of "save" or "save as." You will get a message letting you know that your project was successfully saved. "Save as" will save your project as a new one and keep the old one under its name. You will need to rename your project with the "Save As" option.

It's easy to get so caught up in the design process and anxious to see our finished project that we can forget to hit "save." Your project should automatically save in the cloud, but if it doesn't, you'll have it. It's always better to be safe than sorry.

Now, you've brought your design to your screen. You want to give it a final look and make certain everything is where you want it. If you're ready to cut, click "Make It."

If your Cricut machine isn't turned on, do it now and have all your materials ready. You'll want to follow the prompts. Set your material and load your tools and mat. Press the go icon and wait. When the cutting is done, press unload and carefully remove the mat.

Your project is finished. Wasn't that easy?

Basic Object Editing

The canvas comes equipped with an editing toolbar that allows you to make corrections.

If you make a mistake, you can easily fix it. You can use the "undo" and "redo" buttons by clicking them the required number of times.

The undo icon will let you get rid of something you don't like. It acts as an eraser, and each click will undo the previous action.

If you accidentally delete something, you can use the redo button. This will restore your work.

Another editing tool is the linetype dropdown that will let you change to a cut, draw, or score object. It communicates with your machine, so it knows what tools you're going to be using.

> Linetype   Fill
> Cut ▼   ▢   No Fill ▼   ╱

Cut is the default linetype you'll use unless you've uploaded a JPEG or PNG image. When you click on the "make it" icon, those designs will be cut.

Use Draw if you want to write on your design. You'll be prompted to select a pen, and you'll use this to write or draw.

Tip: This option won't color your designs.

You can use the score feature to score or dash your design.

The edit icon lets you cut, copy, and paste from the canvas. It functions with a dropdown menu, and you use it by selecting the elements you want to edit from your canvas.

The program also features an align tool that will let you move your design around on the canvas. If you've used a design program before, this should be easy for you to do. If you haven't, it can be tricky.

Functions of the Alignment Tool

The following are the functions you can use to move your design on the canvas. You might want to practice using these until you're comfortable with them.

Align allows you to align all of your designs by selecting two or more elements on your canvas.

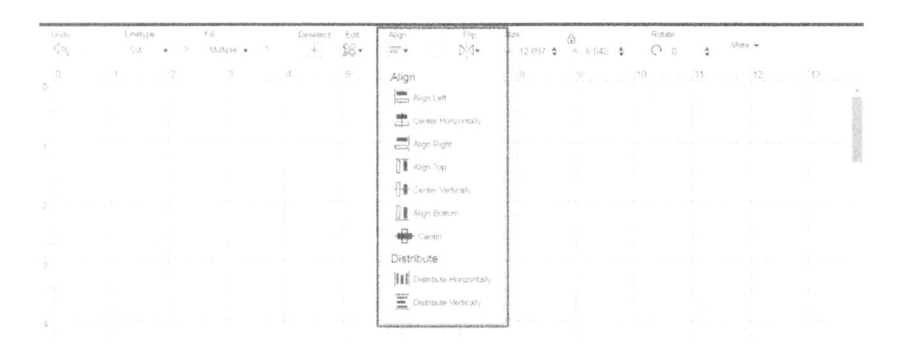

Align Left will move everything to the left.

Center Horizontal will align horizontally and will center text and images. This brings everything to the center.

Align Right will move everything to the right.

Align Top will move the designs you select to the top of the canvas.

Center Vertically will align your selections vertically.

Align Bottom will bring your selections to the bottom.

Center will bring everything to the center, vertically and horizontally.

You can also distribute vertically and horizontally. This will give you some space between your design elements.

You can also flip, arrange, rotate, and size your design. All of these features are handy, and once you master them you can quickly align your design to your preference.

CHAPTER 6:

Ideas with Fabric

Using fabric opens the door to an infinite number of Cricut projects. Whether you like to sew or plan on gluing fabric to things, your machine can cut it for you first. You can revisit the use of heat transfer vinyl as well for further customization. The Cricut Maker is going to be the best machine for most of these projects. The Cricut Explore One and Cricut Explore Air 2 can cut backed fabrics, but the rotary blade on the Maker will be able to cut precisely any fabric without tearing. It is also more powerful, and it can get through thicker and more durable fabrics.

If you have a Cricut Explore One or Cricut Explore Air 2, you will need to bond any fabric you want to cut. The rotary blade in the Cricut Maker can cut any fabric without the need to be bonded. You may be able to use bonded fabrics for some of these projects, but others will require the rotary blade. If you plan to do a lot of work with fabric, it is worth considering an upgrade to the Cricut Maker.

For fabric, you will be using the pink Fabric Grip mat. The fabric will go right side down on the mat—this is the way the Cricut Maker expects it to be, and it cuts the patterns accordingly. If you have the Cricut Washable Fabric Pen, it can make markings before cutting your patterns. The marker will later come out in the wash. A pair of broad tip tweezers will help you pull the fabric off your mat after cutting. Be gentle when you do this so that you don't stretch your fabric. The Fabric Grip mat works a little bit different from the other Cricut cutting mats. The adhesive on it is specially formulated for holding the fabric. It has also been made durable enough to stand up to the additional pressure the Cricut Maker applies. Use a brayer to roll the fabric onto the mat and tweezers to remove it so that the oils from your hands don't damage the adhesive. Never clean your Fabric Grip mat.

Cricut offers printable fabric. You can use your inkjet printer to print designs on this fabric. You can find designs or create your own in Cricut Design Space. This lets you create custom details for your fabric projects. Experiment and see what you can create and print on fabric and how you can use this to add to your projects.

Tassels

Tassels have almost endless uses. These are incredibly easy to make and can be customized to fit whatever purpose you want. Add them to the edges of pillows or blankets, hang them from a string to make a banner, use one as a keychain or zipper pull, and a million other things! You can also try making these with leather or faux leather for a classier look. Tassels are cute on just about everything. For best results, use your Cricut Maker for this project.

Materials:

- 12" x 18" fabric rectangles
- Fabric mat
- Glue gun

Instructions

1. Open Cricut Design Space and create a new project.
2. Select the "Image" button in the lower left-hand corner and search "tassel."
3. Select the image of a rectangle with lines on each side and click "Insert."

4. Place the fabric on the cutting mat.

5. Send the design to the Cricut.

6. Remove the fabric from the mat, saving the extra square.

7. Place the fabric face down and begin rolling tightly, starting on the uncut side. Untangle the fringe as needed.

8. Use some of the scrap fabric and a hot glue gun to secure the tassel at the top.

9. Decorate whatever you want with your new tassels!

Monogrammed Drawstring Bag

Drawstring bags are quick and easy to use. They're just as easy to make! This includes steps for sewing the pieces together, but you could even use fabric glue if you're not great with a needle and thread. You can keep these bags handy for every member of your family to grab and go as needed. You can tell them apart with the monograms, or use a different design on each one to customize them to a certain use, or just decorate it. You can even use these as gift bags! This project uses heat transfer vinyl for the designs, so you'll need your Cricut EasyPress or iron. For best results, use your Cricut Maker for this project.

Materials:

- Two matching rectangles of fabric
- Needle and thread
- Ribbon
- Heat transfer vinyl
- Cricut EasyPress or iron
- Cutting mat
- Weeding tool or pick

Instructions:

1. Open Cricut Design Space and create a new project.
2. Select the "Image" button in the lower left-hand corner and search "monogram."
3. Select the monogram of your choice and click "Insert."

4. Place the iron-on material shiny liner side down on the cutting mat.

5. Send the design to the Cricut.

6. Use the weeding tool or pick to remove excess material.

7. Remove the monogram from the mat.

8. Center the monogram on your fabric, then move it a couple of inches down so that it won't be folded up when the ribbon is drawn.

9. Iron the design onto the fabric.

10. Place the two rectangles together, with the outer side of the fabric facing inward. Sew around the edges, leaving a seam allowance. Leave the top open and stop a couple of inches down from the top.

11. Fold the top of the bag down until you reach your stitches.

12. Sew along the bottom of the folded edge, leaving the sides open.

13. Turn the bag right side out.

14. Thread the ribbon through the loop around the top of the bag.

15. Use your new drawstring bag to carry what you need!

Print Socks

Socks are the ultimate cozy item. No warm pajamas are complete without a pair! Add a cute, hidden accent to the bottom of your or your child's socks with little paw prints. Show off your love for your pet or animals, in general, every time you cuddle up! You can do this with almost any small design or even use text to add a quote to the bottom of your feet. You can use any type of socks you find comfortable. For the easiest read, make sure the sock color and vinyl color contrast. Or make them in the same color for a hidden design! The shine of the vinyl will stand out from the cloth in certain lights. Since this uses heat transfer vinyl, you'll need your Cricut EasyPress or iron. You can use the Cricut Explore One, Cricut Air 2, or Cricut Maker for this project.

Materials:

- Socks
- Heat transfer vinyl
- Cutting mat

- Scrap cardboard

- Weeding tool or pick

- Cricut EasyPress or iron

Instructions

1. Open Cricut Design Space and create a new project.

2. Select the "Image" button in the lower left-hand corner and search "paw prints."

3. Select the paw prints of your choice and click "Insert."

4. Place the iron-on material on the mat.

5. Send the design to the Cricut.

6. Use the weeding tool or pick to remove excess material.

7. Remove the material from the mat.

8. Fit the scrap cardboard inside of the socks.

9. Place the iron-on material on the bottom of the socks.

10. Use the EasyPress to adhere it to the iron-on material.

11. After cooling, remove the cardboard from the socks.

12. Wear your cute paw print socks!

Night Sky Pillow

The night sky is a beautiful thing, and you will love having a piece of it on a cozy pillow. Customize this with the stars you love most, or add constellations, planets, galaxies, and more! Adults and children alike can enjoy these lovely pillows. A sewing machine will make this project a breeze to put together, or you can use a needle and thread. If you're not great at sewing, use fabric glue to close the pillow. Choose a soft fabric that you love so that you can cuddle up with this pillow. You will need your Cricut EasyPress or iron to attach the heat transfer vinyl. You can use the Cricut Explore One, Cricut Explore Air 2, or Cricut Maker for this project.

Materials:

- Black, dark blue, or dark purple fabric
- Heat transfer vinyl in gold or silver
- Cutting mat
- Polyester batting
- Weeding tool or pick
- Cricut EasyPress

Instructions

1. Decide the shape you want for your pillow and cut two matching shapes out of the fabric.
2. Open Cricut Design Space and create a new project.
3. Select the "Image" button in the lower left-hand corner and search "stars."

4. Select the stars of your choice and click "Insert."

5. Place the iron-on material on the mat.

6. Send the design to the Cricut.

7. Use the weeding tool or pick to remove excess material.

8. Remove the material from the mat.

9. Place the iron-on material on the fabric.

10. Use the EasyPress to adhere it to the iron-on material. Sew the two fabric pieces together, leaving an allowance for a seam and a small space. Fill the pillow with polyester batting through the small open space.

11. Sew the pillow shut.

12. Cuddle up to your starry pillow!

Clutch Purse

Clutches are an incredibly useful thing to have around. It is smaller than a regular purse, yet big enough to hold what you need, and you can use them for any occasion. Create a few of these in different colors and patterns to match different outfits! This clutch is inspired by a project that Cricut has in the Design Space. It is the most advanced of the fabric projects in this book, and it uses the most sewing. For the best results, use the Cricut Maker for this project.

Materials

- Two fabrics, one for the exterior and one for the interior
- Fusible fleece
- Fabric cutting mat
- D-ring
- Sew-on snap

- Lace

- Zipper

- Sewing machine

- Fabric scissors

- Keychain or charm of your choice

Instructions

1. Open Cricut Design Space and create a new project.

2. Select the "Image" button in the lower left-hand corner and search for "essential wallet."

3. Select the essential wallet template and click "Insert."

4. Place the fabric on the mat.

5. Send the design to the Cricut.

6. Remove the fabric from the mat.

7. Attach the fusible fleecing to the wrong side of the exterior fabric.

8. Attach lace to the edges of the exterior fabric.

9. Assemble the D-ring strap.

10. Place the D-ring onto the strap and sew into place.

11. Fold the pocket pieces wrong side out over the top of the zipper and sew it into place.

12. Fold the pocket's wrong side in and sew the sides.

13. Sew the snap in the pocket.

14. Lay the pocket on the right side of the main fabric lining so that the corners of the pocket's bottom are behind the curved edges of the lining fabric. Sew the lining piece to the zipper tape.

15. Fold the lining behind the pocket and iron in place.

16. Sew on the other side of the snap.

17. Trim the zipper so that it's not overhanging the edge.

18. Sew the two pocket layers to the exterior fabric across the bottom.

19. Sew around all of the layers.

20. Trim the edges with fabric scissors.

21. Turn the clutch almost completely inside out and sew the opening closed.

22. Turn the clutch all the way inside out and press the corners into place.

23. Attach your charm or keychain to the zipper.

24. Carry your new clutch wherever you need it!

CHAPTER 7:

Ideas with Glass

Etched Glass Casserole Dish

Project inspired by Hello Creative Family

If you are responsible for bringing food to a party, why not make it personal? Add a little message to the bottom of your dish, or your name, to make sure your host knows that you appreciate the invitation and who to return the dish to when it is done!

You'll need:

- 9x13" glass baking dish
- Etching cream and application brush
- Stencil vinyl
- Rubber gloves
- Transfer Tape

Step 1

In Design Space, add your words and graphics that you want to have cut from the stencil vinyl. In this example, the words are "Eat, Drink, Be Merry" with a spoon and fork image. Adjust them to fit on the bottom of the dish, no bigger than 12" or wider than 8". Make sure to mirror your design for easier application!

Step 2

Once your design is laid out, click on "Make It" and follow the prompts to cut it from the stencil vinyl.

Step 3

Weed out your design, and using your transfer tape, place the negative vinyl onto the bottom of your baking dish.

Make sure to use your scraper to get the sticky side of the stencil to attach smoothly to the bottom of your dish, paying close attention to the little parts of the design. Also, do not place the image on the bottom of the dish where food will be placed, but rather on the underside of the dish, so it shows through the glass but does not come in contact with food.

Step 4

Remove the transfer tape and follow the directions on the bottle of etching cream you purchased. Wear your rubber gloves and use your application brush! Let dry appropriately.

Step 5

Keeping your rubber gloves on, remove the excess etching cream. This usually requires washing it off in the sink with a paper towel or soft cloth. Pat dry and then peel off the stencil. Enjoy!

Superhero Beer or Drinking Glasses

Project inspired by I am Momma Hear Me Roar

Capture the attention and the heart of your superhero-loving friend or partner with a set of these custom beer or drinking glasses. It is easy to do and inexpensive, too! Check the dollar store for the perfect glass to work with if you do not have some already!

You'll need:

- Several smooth, glass drinking glasses
- Etching cream and application brush
- Stencil vinyl
- Rubber gloves
- Transfer Tape

Step 1

In Design Space, search for superhero logos. Remove the extra layers, so they are only the outlines. Make as many logos as your glasses count. This means if you have six glasses, choose six logos to print. Send your file to cut on the stencil vinyl by clicking on "Make It." Follow the prompts to cut. Do not forget to mirror your images!

Step 2

Once your images are cut in the vinyl, weed out the interior pieces, making sure to keep the little pieces intact! Working with one logo at a time, transfer the logo with the transfer tape to a glass. Use your scraper tool to make sure there are no air bubbles, and it is firmly attached to the glass. Repeat this for each logo.

Step 3

Remove the transfer tape and follow the instructions on your etching cream. Allow drying at the appropriate time. Make sure to use your rubber gloves and application brush.

Step 4

Wearing your rubber gloves, wash off the excess etching cream with a paper towel or soft, clean cloth. Pat dry and remove the vinyl carefully. Now get ready for awe and appreciation!

Etched Monogrammed Glass

Glasses are one of the most-used things in your kitchen, and it's impossible to have too many of them. It's actually quite easy to customize them with etching, and it will look as if a professional did it. Simply use glass etching cream that you can find at any craft store! Be sure to read the instructions and warning labels carefully before you begin. The vinyl will act as a stencil, protecting the parts of the glass that you don't want to etch. Be sure to take your time to get the vinyl smooth against the glass, especially where there are small bits. You don't want any of the cream to get under the edge of the vinyl. You can use the Cricut Explore One, Cricut Explore Air 2, or Cricut Maker for this project.

Supplies Needed

- A glass of your choice – make sure that the spot you want to monogram is smooth
- Vinyl
- Cutting mat
- Weeding tool or pick
- Glass etching cream

Instructions

1. Open Cricut Design Space and create a new project.
2. Select the "Image" button in the Design Panel and search for "monogram."
3. Select your preferred monogram and click "Insert."

4. Put your vinyl on the cutting mat.

5. Send the design to the Cricut.

6. Use the weeding tool or pick to remove the monogram, leaving the vinyl around it.

7. Remove the vinyl from the mat.

8. Carefully apply the vinyl around your glass, making it as smooth as possible, particularly around the monogram.

9. If you have any letters with holes in your monogram, carefully reposition those cutouts in their proper place.

10. Following the instructions on the etching cream, apply it to your monogram.

11. Remove the cream and then the vinyl.

12. Give your glass a good wash.

13. Enjoy drinking out of your etched glass!

Live, Love, Laugh Glass Block

Glass blocks are an inexpensive yet surprisingly versatile craft material. You can find them at both craft and hardware stores. They typically have a hole with a lid so that you can fill the blocks with the items of your choice.

This project uses tiny fairy lights for a glowing quote block, but you can fill it however you'd like. The frost spray paint adds a bit of elegance to the glass and diffuses the light for a softer glow, hiding the string of the fairy lights.

Holographic vinyl will add to the magical look, but you can use whatever colors you'd like.

This features a classic quote that's great to have around your house, but you can change it. You can use the Cricut Explore One, Cricut Explore Air 2, or Cricut Maker for this project.

Supplies Needed

- Glass block
- Frost spray paint
- Clear enamel spray
- Holographic vinyl
- Vinyl transfer tape
- Cutting mat
- Weeding tool or pick
- Fairy lights

Instructions

1. Spray the entire glass block with frost spray paint and let it dry.
2. Spray the glass block with a coat of clear enamel spray and let it dry.
3. Open Cricut Design Space and create a new project.
4. Select the "Text" button in the Design Panel.
5. Type "Live Love Laugh" in the text box.
6. Use the dropdown box to select your favorite font.
7. Arrange the words to sit on top of each other.
8. Place your vinyl on the cutting mat.
9. Send the design to your Cricut.
10. Use a weeding tool or pick to remove the excess vinyl from the design.
11. Apply transfer tape to the design.
12. Remove the paper backing and apply the words to the glass block.
13. Smooth down the design and carefully remove the transfer tape.
14. Place fairy lights in the opening of the block, leaving the battery pack on the outside.
15. Enjoy your decorative quote!

Unicorn Wine Glass

Who doesn't love unicorns? Who doesn't love wine? Bring them together with these glittery wine glasses! The outdoor vinyl will hold up to use and washing, and the Mod Podge will keep the glitter in place for years to come. Customize it even more with your own quote. You could use a different magical creature as well—mermaids go great with glitter too! Customize this to suit your tastes or to create gifts for your friends and family. Consider using these for a party and letting the guests take them home as favors! You can use the Cricut Explore One, Cricut Explore Air 2, or Cricut Maker for this project.

Supplies Needed

- Stemless wine glasses
- Outdoor vinyl in the color of your choice
- Vinyl transfer tape
- Cutting mat
- Weeding tool or pick
- Extra fine glitter in the color of your choice
- Mod Podge

Instructions

1. Open Cricut Design Space and create a new project.

2. Select the "Text" button in the Design Panel.

3. Type "It's not drinking alone if my unicorn is here."

4. Using the dropdown box, select your favorite font.

5. Adjust the positioning of the letters, rotating some to give a whimsical look.

6. Select the "Image" button on the Design Panel and search for "unicorn."

7. Select your favorite unicorn and click "Insert," then arrange your design as desired on the glass.

8. Place your vinyl on the cutting mat, making sure it is smooth and making full contact.

9. Send the design to your Cricut.

10. Use a weeding tool or pick to remove the excess vinyl from the design. Use the Cricut BrightPad to help if you have one.

11. Apply transfer tape to the design, pressing firmly, and making sure there are no bubbles.

12. Remove the paper backing and apply the words to the glass where you'd like them. Leave at least a couple of inches at the bottom for the glitter.

13. Smooth down the design and carefully remove the transfer tape.

14. Coat the bottom of the glass in Mod Podge, wherever you would like glitter to be. Give the area a wavy edge.

15. Sprinkle glitter over the Mod Podge, working quickly before it dries.

16. Add another layer of Mod Podge and glitter, and set it aside to dry.

17. Cover the glitter in a thick coat of Mod Podge.

18. Allow the glass to cure for at least 48 hours.

19. Enjoy drinking from your unicorn wine glass!

Window Decoration

Materials needed – "Cricut Maker" or "Cricut Explore," cutting mat, orange window cling (non-adhesive material that has static cling so it can be easily applied on the glass; since it does not have sticky cling like vinyl, make sure you put this on the inner side of the window to protect exposure from external weather).

Step 1

Log into the "Design Space" application and click on the "New Project" button on the top right corner of the screen to view a blank canvas.

Step 2

Click on the "Projects" icon click on the "All Categories" to select "Home Decor," then type in "window" in the search bar.

Step 3

Click on "Customize" to edit the project to your preference further, or click on the "Make It" button and load the window cling to your "Cricut" machine and follow the instructions on the screen to cut your project and transfer onto the window.

CHAPTER 8:

Ideas with Vinyl

Christmas Ornaments

Project inspired by Hey Let's Make Stuff

If you are not thinking about the holidays in November and December, you are missing a great opportunity. It is never too early to think about gift giving. Use your Cricut machine to make gifts and decorations that everyone will enjoy.

You'll need:

- Adhesive vinyl
- Adhesive foil
- Cricut Pens
- Ornaments - plain or clear are good options

Step 1

In Design Space, upload your preferred design, image, or create your own with custom shapes.

To make a dimensional design, add various layers, and consider using different materials and colors to get a professional appearance.

If you want to cut words out and attach them to a strip of vinyl in another color, you can wrap that around your design. Or you could layer different vinyl, one solid and the other glitter.

Step 2

Carefully lay out your vinyl where you want it to appear on your ornament and transfer the vinyl to the ornament. Transfer tape is best for this type of project. You can use a measuring tape or ruler and a marking pen to help you find the central location for best results.

Step 3

You can have vinyl and designs attached directly to the ornaments, or you can consider having pieces that hang on the outside or off of it as well. This can be a fun and personal gift, but the more you do it and practice working on a round surface, the better you will get at it!

Mason Jar Tags

Project inspired by Creativebug

Jammers rejoice! This customized label allows you to give your homemade food creations a little extra "oomph." They are incredibly easy and can fit any jar you want to use.

You'll need:

- Adhesive Vinyl in lighter colors like white or yellow
- Weeding Tool
- Transfer Tape
- Mason Jars

Step 1

Clean your jars well, especially the outside where you want to place your label. Removing as much prior residue as possible will help your new labels stick better. Also, measure the circumference and height of your jars. This way, you know which jar label canvas you need to create.

Step 2

In Design Space, open a new canvas based on the size of your mason jar that you want to create the labels for. Typically, there is a pre-set canvas. If you do not find a canvas that is the right size, open the one closest to your measurements and adjust from there.

Upload the desired images to your canvas and add any words you want to appear on the label. This can include a special message or describe the contents of the jar, etc. Make sure to detach your images so it will appear properly on your labels.

Step 3

After laying out your images and words, go back and attach all the pieces together and send your file to cut.

Step 4

After your labels are cut, weed out any unnecessary pieces and remove the excess vinyl you do not want to use. Apply the transfer tape to the vinyl and then remove the backing. Using the transfer tape, adhere the vinyl to the clean exterior of your mason jar. Smooth it with your scraper tool, and then slowly peel back the tape.

Cork Coasters

Project inspired by Sewbon

Personalize your home with this sweet little project or give a gift for a housewarming party or holiday. You can do abstract designs and words like the example or make it more personal with photos and images if you want.

You'll need:

- Cork for cutting on your Cricut
- Adhesive Vinyl
- Adhesive Felt or felt tabs
- Transfer Tape

Step 1

In Design Space, decide what size and shape of a coaster you want to create. Traditional coasters are often circular or square, but like the example shows, you do not need to be bound to those shapes for your coasters. Make sure you also have the quantity you plan to make in mind.

Step 2

When you have your design laid out, send the bottom shapes to cut out of the cork material.

Step 3

Once your cork is cut, use the coaster shapes in Design Space to now design the images, words, or other details to your coasters. You can make each coaster the same design, or you can use a theme and create custom messages for each one. It can be nice to add dates, monograms, and photographs instead of shapes and sayings. Make sure whatever you decide will fit on the coasters you just cut out. Once you have these laid out, send your file to cut from the colored vinyl you have chosen. Weed out any unnecessary parts and then use transfer tape to move your vinyl from its backing to your project. Smooth out the vinyl with your scraper tool before removing the tape.

Step 4

Using an Exacto knife, lay your coasters on top of the adhesive felt and cut around the shape. Peel off the backing and apply the felt to the underside of the coaster. If you are using felt tabs instead, make sure there is a tab at least at every corner or few inches on your coaster's bottom. If you want a raise coaster, you could even cut designs from the felt and add them over the vinyl on top! It is not necessary to add the felt pieces on the bottom of the cork, but it does add a more professional touch to your project. It also adds extra protection for your furniture where you will be using the coasters.

Embellished Shoes

Project inspired by Moon Creations

There is no need to settle for "boring" or "average'" shoes anymore. And no need to let your child suffer from not knowing what foot goes to what shoe any more with this project. Adding a simple vinyl phrase or image to the soles of your shoes or even the top if you have a canvas shoe can make a big difference. To achieve this look, you will want to duplicate any images or phrases you choose or remember to make designs for both shoes, not just one!

You'll need:

- Shoes to embellish - Canvas is not necessary unless you want to iron on something to the top.

- Adhesive vinyl or iron-vinyl, depending on your design and shoe

- Transfer tape and scraper tool

- Iron, if required for iron-on

Step 1

In Design Space, create your image or phrase and send the file to cut out of the vinyl. You can use the phrase for one shoe and the negative vinyl for the other, or you can send the file to cut two times.

Step 2

Use the transfer tape to remove the vinyl design and line it up on the shoe where you want to put it. Using the scraper tool, smooth the vinyl on the shoe. If you add an iron-on design, heat your iron and place your vinyl on the shoe's canvas portion. Place a cloth over the top and iron it on.

Step 3

Carefully peel away the backing of the vinyl, making sure it has completely attached to the shoe. You can go back over your vinyl with the iron or scraper tool to ensure everything is securely in place.

Step 4

Throw on your new custom shoes and show them off to the world!

CRICUT PROJECT IDEAS

Chipboard puzzle

Project inspired by Jen Goode

When you need a fast present for a party or want to share a special moment, or need to send a unique message to someone, a puzzle is a great option. Use this lovely puzzle design to make anything a bit more mysterious and special.

You can develop your own design in Design Space or upload an image already present if you want. You can do just about anything from a pregnancy announcement to the alphabet.

You'll need:

- Chipboard
- Adhesive vinyl
- Ruler
- Masking or painter's tape

Step 1

Open Design Space and upload the image you want for your project. Make sure to create your canvas to the size of the puzzle you want to make and adjust your image to fit accordingly. There is a puzzle canvas in Design Space that you can use for the project or develop your puzzle cuts. If this is your first time creating the project, try out the present cut file to get used to the process.

Step 2

Send your file to print and cut. This will first print on your vinyl and then cut the square out for the project.

Step 3

Next, you will want to place your chipboard on your cutting mat. To make sure it is secured well, use a few strips of tape to hold it on your mat for cutting. Make marks on the chipboard before cutting one inch in on all sides. This will help you when placing your vinyl. Also, if you have a StrongGrip mat, use it for this part of the project.

Step 4

Before sending your project to cut, transfer your vinyl to the chipboard, aligning it with the marks you just made, so it is in the center of the board. Go over your vinyl with your scraper tool to make sure it adheres properly.

Step 5

Adjust your cutting blade for the chipboard and then send the puzzle file to cut. This will make sure the chipboard and vinyl are cut at the same time and are seamlessly aligned. If the project does not cut away the outside one-inch margin, consider painting it a corresponding color. Still, it should be trimmed away in the process.

Shoes Pouch

Project inspired by Atta Girl Says

Maybe it is for going to the gym, yoga, or dance, a shoe pouch is great for keeping both shoes together and neat. Plus, it makes a great gift for someone you know needs a little stylish organization in their life. You can sew this project together using a serger or straight stitch machine, or you can use liquid stitches or adhesive hem tape to enclose your project if you are not a sewer.

You'll need:

- ½ yard of the desired fabric
- Ribbon
- Thread for stitching, needle if you are doing it by hand, or another "sewing" method like liquid stitches or fusible hem tape.

- Iron-on vinyl

- Sewing materials: scissors, rotary cutter, clear quilting ruler, pins, fray check, fabric marking pen

- Iron

Step 1

Use your ruler and rotary cutter to cut the fabric in the size you want.

For soft shoes, consider a rectangle like 12" by 9". For larger shoes, use maybe a rectangle about 24" by 12." Apply fray check to the edges of your fabric.

Step 2

Use your ruler to mark two spots on your fabric, 1 ½ inches from the top on each side.

Step 3

Open Design Space and prepare the image and words for your bag. Make sure your canvas is set to ½ the width of your fabric to account for the fold in the fabric.

This means you do not want anything that is larger than 9" or 12" or wider than 6" or 12" depending on your fabric rectangle's size.

Once you have your image laid out, make sure to mirror your image before sending it to cut.

Step 4

Cut your vinyl and make sure to weed away any small parts you do not want.

Step 5

Lay out your vinyl on your fabric, sticky side down on the print side of your fabric. Do not lay your design about ½" from the bottom or sides of your fabric to account for the seam you will create. Also, keep it about one inch from the top to account for the ribbon loop you are going to create. Once you have it laid out, use a pressing cloth and your iron to attach your vinyl to your fabric.

Step 6

After you adhere your vinyl to your project, fold your fabric in half and align the edges, pinning them in place. Sew along the edge to secure the bag shape. If you are using another means of making the bag, follow the directions on the packaging. Make sure to fold the fabric in ½ inch to enclose the raw edges of the fabric. Do not sew or close off the top of your bag. Also, do not sew beyond the markings you made with your pen earlier.

Step 7

Fold the edge of the top of your bag down. You can make a little fold, about ¼ inch, and then fold again at ¾ inch to encase the seam allowance, or just fold it down one inch and sew it closed. Again, if you are not sewing your project, use your closure material to create the ribbon casing for closing the bag. Do not close off the ends of the bag, making a tube for the ribbon to pass through.

Step 8

Cut a length of ribbon three or more inches longer than the unfinished width of your bag, meaning 15" or "28". Apply fray check to the ends of the ribbon. Thread the ribbon through the ribbon casing or tube you just created.

Attaching a safety pin to one end of the ribbon and using it to pass the ribbon through can help this process. You want the ribbon coming out on one side of the bag for you can clinch it closed and tie a bow to keep the shoes inside.

Step 9

Consider adding a new pair of shoes or a special treat inside the bag if you give it as a gift, or simply slide your shoes on and take them with you in their stylish new casing!

Sleeping Mask

Project inspired by Bespoke Bride

Another "sewing" project that you can make with your Cricut is a sleeping mask to help block out unwanted light. These are great for traveling and times when you need some shut-eye, but the sun is still shining. Like the previous project, you can sew this with a sewing machine or serger, or you can use liquid stitching or iron-on hem tape to capture the look you are going for.

You'll need:

- Printed or solid top fabric, such as cotton quilting fabric
- Silky or Minky fabric for the underside of the mask that sits over your eyes
- 13 inches of wide, good-quality elastic
- iron-on vinyl in the corresponding color, like black
- Sewing materials: scissors, rotary cutter, clear quilting ruler, pins, fray check, fabric marking pen

Step 1

To begin, start with the vinyl image you want on the outside of your eye mask. This can be a word or a graphic. Design the image on Design Space, making sure that the image will fit on an eye mask. In general, you do not want an image longer than four inches or higher than two inches. Once you have your design laid out, send the file to be cut from your vinyl. When the image is done cutting, weed it if necessary, and prepare it to be transferred to the eye mask.

Step 2

If you are making your mask by hand, create the eye mask pattern on paper. You can also do this in Cricut, making the eye mask shape and cutting it on paper. Lay your pattern over your two different fabrics, placing the right sides of the fabrics together. Pin the pattern down and cut it out with a rotary cutter. If you want your custom mask, use your face measurements to adjust your pattern.

Step 3

Once you have your top mask cut out, lay your vinyl design on it and press it onto the mask. Make sure to use the "cotton" setting on your iron and place a pressing cloth or a soft, clean cloth in between your design and the iron. Before you remove the backing, make sure your vinyl is fully transferred. Once the backing is removed, pass your iron over the design one more time.

Step 4

Lay the bottom, minky, or silky fabric on the cutting table with the fashion side or right side of the fabric facing you. Pin one end of the elastic to one side of the material in the center of the eye mask and then bring the other end to the opposite side of the mask, pinning that end in place, too. Pin it, so the end is facing out of your fabric. Let about one inch of the elastic hang over the edge on each side.

Once the elastic is secured, place your top fabric with the vinyl design on top of the minky or silky fabric, placing the design down away from you. Use more pins to attach the two pieces of fabric together and prepare the project for sewing. If you are not sewing your project, skip directly to the alternative step.

Step 5

Using your sewing machine or a needle and thread, stitch the edges of your eye mask together, leaving a two-inch space on the top, straight edge of your mask. Keep the opening at least one inch away from your elastic—the further, the better. Make sure to back stitch over the elastic area to give it more support.

Step 6

When you are done sewing, turn your project right side out by pressing it through the open space you left open. Your mask should look almost complete, but with a two-inch gap still visible. Press the edges of the opening inside the mask and use a needle and thread to close the mask's hole. If you press it with an iron first, it will help keep all the loose and raw edges contained while sewing it closed. If you want to add a decorative top stitch to your design, stitch around ¼ inch from the edge. This will also stabilize your design. Once you are done, press with an iron.

Amended Step

For those that do not want to sew the project, you can press the raw edges in on the minky and fashion fabric with your iron.

Use a piece of fusible interfacing cut out in the shape of the eye mask but trimmed by ½ inch around the edges. Lay that on the wrong side of your minky or silky fabric and place your fashion fabric on top, with the design facing you.

Set your iron on the fabric, with a pressing cloth in between. Add extra interfacing to where you inserted the elastic to add more stability. Make sure the interfacing fully adheres the layers together and that the elastic is secured in place.

Vinyl Wall Decals

Materials:

- Adhesive vinyl
- Cricut machine
- Weeding tool
- Scrapper tool

Instructions

1. Log in to the Cricut design space.
2. Create a new project.
3. Click on Upload Image.

4. Drag the image to the design space.
5. Highlight the image and "flatten" it.
6. Click on the Make It button.
7. Place vinyl on the cutting mat.
8. Custom dial the machine to vinyl.
9. Load the cutting mat into the machine.
10. Push the mat up against the rollers.
11. Cut the design out of the vinyl.
12. Weed out the excess vinyl with a weeding tool.
13. Apply a thin layer of transfer tape on the vinyl.
14. Peel off the backing.
15. Apply the transfer tape on the wall.
16. Smoothen with a scraper tool to let out the air bubble.
17. Carefully peel off the transfer tape from the wall.

Vinyl Easter Eggs

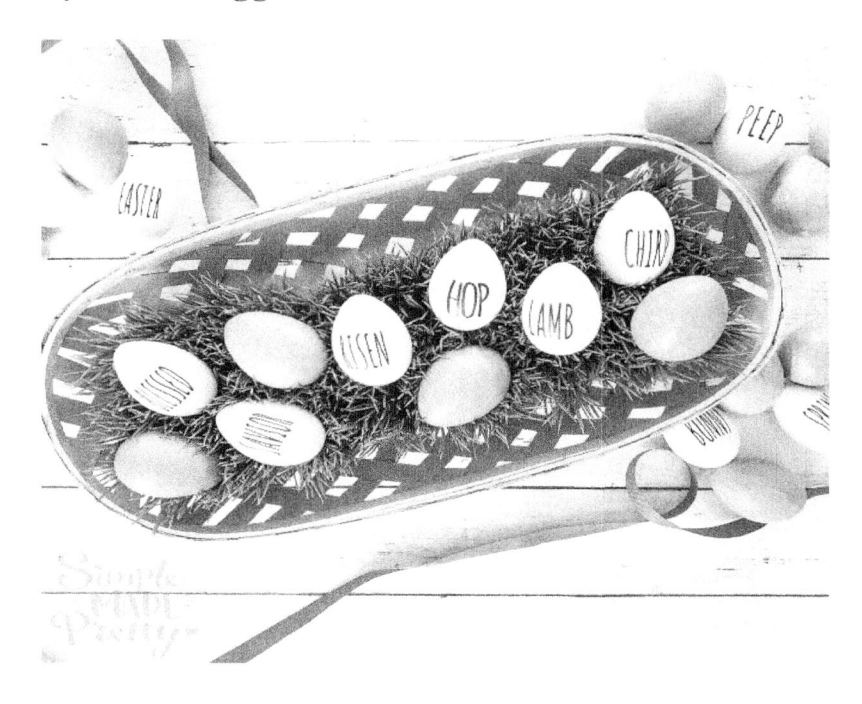

You may have a Rae Dunn obsession like me. So, I have been able to create these Rea Dunn inspired Easter Eggs. Because we are aware that the Rae Dunn products have become increasingly popular over the years on the blown-up craft blogs and websites. You would need the Cricut machine to do these, and it is easy. This is a very useful project during a festive period like Easter.

Materials

- The Cricut Explore machine
- Contact Papers
- The White Craft Eggs
- Vinyl (The Easter eggs are white, so I used black)

STEP 1

Get a free SVG, PNG, DXF file online, or you just create one yourself. Upload to the Cricut Design Space. And gather your supplies. I got these Easter eggs for just $2.

STEP 2

Make some little tweaks to the design in the design space. You should remember that the design measurement should be very small to match the size of the egg. I made use of 1 x 1 inch for all the eggs. Then you weed out the cut images too.

STEP 3

Spread over your contact paper and adhere them to the eggs.

STEP 4

Peel off the contact paper to expose the egg.

Repeat the same process for the remaining eggs.

Vinyl Sticker Car Window

Materials:

- Cricut machine
- Premium outdoor glossy vinyl
- Transfer tape
- Scraper tool

Instructions:

1. Get and save the image you want to use online.
2. Log in to the Cricut design space and start a new project.
3. Click on the Upload icon and upload the saved image.
4. Click on the image and drag to the next page, then select the image type.
5. Select the parts of the image you do not want as part of the final cut.

6. Select the image as a cute image. You will get to preview the image as a cut image.

7. Approve the cut image. You would be redirected to the first upload screen.

8. Click on your just finished cut file, then highlight it and insert the image.

9. The image is added to your design space for size readjusting. The image is ready to cut.

10. Cut the image and remove excessive vinyl after the image is cut.

11. Apply a layer of transfer tape to the top of the cut vinyl.

12. Clean the car window really well with rubbing alcohol to remove all dirt.

13. Carefully peel away the paperback of the vinyl.

14. Apply the cut vinyl on the window. Start at one end and roll it down.

15. Go over the applied vinyl with a scraper tool to remove the air bubble underneath the vinyl.

16. Slowly peel away the transfer tape from the window.

Bed And Breakfast Guest Room Wood Sign

Supplies:

- Vinyl
- Electronic cutting machine
- FolkArt Color shift Acrylic Paint (Aqua Flash)
- Painted panels
- The paintbrush

Instructions

- Vinyl is used as a stencil, and therefore the color does not matter.
- You will weed out the positive space instead of weeding out the negative space.

- Paint all the pieces you want.

- When finished, rub it on top and remove the vinyl back.

- Rub it with the squeegee.

- Put the wood mark on it and rub the squeegee gently, then take out the transfer ribbon.

- The paintbrush could get too close to the edges of the wood's surface.

- The Acrylic Paint of FolkArt ® Color Shift is very fun.

- Squeeze out some on a palette, or just peel off a little of the vinyl backrest.

- Tap onto the paint and dab on a palette the stencil brush.

- You don't want a paintbrush loaded or underneath the vinyl stencil to seep it.

- Take the whole positive space up and down.

- FolkArt ® Color Shift Acrylic Paint has a certain texture when applied, and a second cover is applied.

- Allow the paint to dry then.

- This is a questionable point. Some people like to wet paint and stencils, but honestly, it just requires wet paint to be scrubbed everywhere! Let it dry. Let it dry.

- Then in a corner, peel the vinyl. Peel it back over the top, just as it rolls over it.

- Watch now! Now! It is perfection! B&B— you make both of you!

- I'm thrilled... thick paint raises words and pops.

- That would make for a hostess a great gift too!

- Are you not loving it? Have you got the right spot for such a sign?

- Get to the lobby and collect one supply!

Wooden Hand-Lettered Sign

Hand-lettered wooden signs are a wonderful way to utilize your Cricut for creative projects.

What you will need:

- Acrylic paint for whatever colors you would like
- Vinyl
- Cricut Explore Air 2
- Walnut hollow basswood planks
- Transfer Tape
- Scraper
- An SVG file or font that you wish to use
- Pencil
- Eraser

Instructions:

1. You will need to start by deciding what you will want to draw onto the wood.

2. Then, place some lines on the plank to designate the horizontal and vertical axis for the grid. Set this aside for later.

3. Upload the file that you wish to use to the Design Space. Then cut the file with the proper setting for vinyl.

4. Weed out the writing or design spaces that are not meant to go on the wood.

5. Using the transfer tape, apply the tape to the top of the vinyl and smooth it out. Using the scraper and the transfer paper's corner, slowly peel the backing off a bit at a time. Do it carefully.

6. Remove the backing of the vinyl pieces, aligning the lettering or design so that it is fully centered. Place it carefully on the wooden plank.

7. Again, use the scraper to smooth out the vinyl on the plank.

8. Take off the transfer tape by smoothing off the bubbles as you scrape the wood sign. Discard the transfer tape at that time.

9. Continue to use the scraper to make the vinyl smoother. There should be no bumps since this creates bleeding.

10. Now, paint your wood plank with any color of your choice. Peel the vinyl letters off. Once the paint has completely dried, you are able to erase your pencil marks.

CHAPTER 9:

Ideas with Paper

It is ideal to start your first project using paper-based designs since these projects are easier to design and cut. You can get professional looking results with minimum investment. You will learn to create a variety of projects that you can further customize as you follow the instructions below and have unique designs of your own.

Recipe Stickers

Materials

- "Cricut Maker" or "Cricut Explore"
- Sticker paper and cutting mat.

Instructions

Step 1

Log into the "Design Space" application and click on the "New Project" button on the top right corner of the screen to view a blank canvas.

Step 2

Click on the "Images" icon on the "Design Panel" and type in "stickers" in the search bar.

Click on the desired image and then click on the "Insert Images" button at the bottom of the screen.

Step 3

The selected image will be displayed on the canvas. It can be edited using applicable tools from the "Edit Image Bar." You can make multiple changes to the image as you need, for example, you could change the color of the image or change its size (sticker should be between 2-4 inches wide). The image selected for this project has words "stickers" inside the design, so let's delete that by first clicking on the "Ungroup" button and selecting the "Stickers" layer, and clicking on the red "x" button. Click on the "Text" button and type in the name of your recipe, as shown in the picture below.

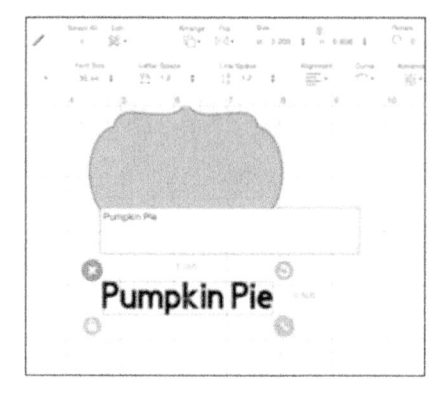

Step 4

Drag and drop the text in the middle of the design and select the entire design. Now, click on "Align" and select "Center Horizontally" and "Center Vertically."

Step 5

Select the entire design and click on the "Group" icon on the top right of the screen under "Layers panel." Now, copy and paste the designs and update the text for all your recipes.

Tip - Use your keyboard shortcut "Ctrl + C" and "Ctrl + V" to copy and paste the design.

Step 6

Click on "Save" at the top right corner of the screen to name and save your project.

Step 7

To cut your design, just click on the "Make It" button on the screen's top right corner. Load the sticker paper to your "Cricut" machine and click "Continue" at the bottom right corner of the screen to start cutting your design.

Note – The "Continue" button will only appear after you have purchased images and fonts that are available for purchase only.

Step 8

Set your cut setting to "Vinyl" (recommended for sticker paper, since it tends to be thicker than regular paper). Place the sticker paper on top of the cutting mat and follow the screen prompts to finish cutting your design. Viola! You have your own customized recipe stickers.

Custom Notebooks

Materials needed

- "Cricut Maker" or "Cricut Explore"
- Cutting mat
- Washi sheets or your choice of decorative paper/ crepe paper/ fabric.

Instructions

Step 1

Log into the "Design Space" application and click on the "New Project" button on the top right corner of the screen to view a blank canvas.

Step 2

Using an already existing project from the "Cricut" library and customize it. So click on the "Projects" icon on the "Design Panel" and type in "notebook" in the search bar.

Step 3

Click on "Customize" so you can further edit the project to your preference. For example, the "unicorn notebook" project is shown below. You can click on the "Linetype Swatch" to change the color of the design.

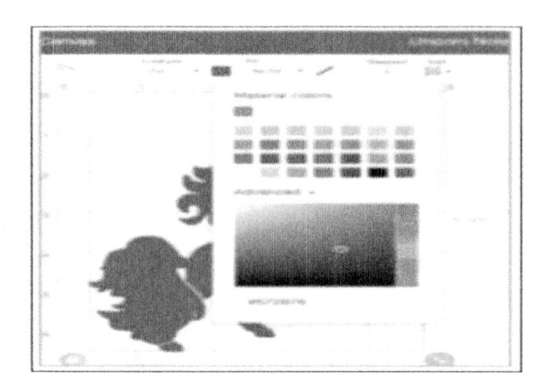

Step 4

The design is ready to be cut. Simply click on the "Make It" button and load the washi paper sheet to your "Cricut" machine and follow the instructions on the screen to cut your project.

Paper Flowers

Materials needed

- "Cricut Maker" or "Cricut Explore"
- Cutting Mat
- Cardstock
- Adhesive

Instructions

Step 1

Log into the "Design Space" application and click on the "New Project" button on the screen's top right corner to view a blank canvas.

Step 2

Click on the "Images" icon on the "Design Panel" and type in "flower" in the search bar.

Click on the desired image, then click on the "Insert Images" button at the bottom of the screen.

Step 3

The selected image will be displayed on the canvas and can be edited using applicable tools from the "Edit Image Bar."

Then copy and paste the flower five times and make them a size smaller than the preceding flower to create a variable size for depth and texture for the design, as shown in the picture below.

Step 4

The design is ready to be cut. Simply click on the "Make It" button and load the cardstock to your "Cricut" machine and follow the screen's instructions to cut your project.

Step 5

Once the design has been cut, simply remove the cut flowers and bend them at the center. Then using the adhesive, stack flowers with the largest flowers at the bottom.

Crepe Paper Bouquet

Materials

- "Cricut Maker" or "Cricut Explore"
- Standard grip mat
- Crepe paper in desired colors
- Floral wire
- Floral tape
- Hot glue
- Fern fronds
- Vase

Instructions

Step 1

Log into the "Design Space" application and click on the "New Project" button on the top right corner of the screen to view a blank canvas.

Step 2

Let's use an already existing project from the "Cricut" library and customize it.

So click on the "Projects" icon and type in "crepe bouquet" in the search bar.

Step 3

Click on "Customize" so you can further edit the project to your preference, or simply click on the "Make It" button and load the crepe paper to your "Cricut" machine and follow the instructions on the screen to cut your project.

Step 4

To assemble the design, follow the assembly instructions provided under the "Assemble" section of the project details, as shown in the picture below.

Leaf Banner

Materials

- "Cricut Maker" or "Cricut Explore"
- Standard grip mat
- Watercolor paper and paint
- Felt balls
- Needle and thread
- Hot glue

Instructions

Step 1

Log into the "Design Space" application and click on the "New Project" button on the top right corner of the screen to view a blank canvas.

Step 2

Let's use an already existing project from the "Cricut" library and customize it.

So click on the "Projects" icon and type in "leaf banner" in the search bar.

Step 3

Click on "Customize" so you can further edit the project to your preference, or simply click on the "Make It" button and load the watercolor paper to your "Cricut" machine and follow the instructions on the screen to cut your project.

Step 4

Use watercolors to paint the leaves and let them dry completely. Then create a garland using the needle and thread through the felt balls and sticking the leaves to the garland with hot glue.

Paper Pinwheels

Materials

- "Cricut Maker" or "Cricut Explore"
- Standard grip mat
- Patterned cardstock in desired colors
- Embellishments
- Paper straws
- Hot glue

Instructions

Step 1

Log into the "Design Space" application and click on the "New Project" button on the top right corner of the screen to view a blank canvas.

Step 2

Let's use an already existing project from the "Cricut" library and customize it.

So click on the "Projects" icon and type in "paper pinwheel" in the search bar.

Step 3

Click on "Customize" to edit the project to your preference further, or simply click on the "Make It" button and load the cardstock to your "Cricut" machine and follow the instructions on the screen to cut your project.

Step 4

Using hot glue, adhere the pinwheels together to the paper straws and the embellishment, as shown in the picture below:

Paper Lollipops

Materials

- "Cricut Maker" or "Cricut Explore"
- LightGrip mat
- Patterned cardstock in desired colors
- Glitter
- Wooden dowels
- Hot glue

Instructions

Step 1

Log into the "Design Space" application and click on the "New Project" button on the screen's top right corner to view a blank canvas.

Step 2

Let's use an already existing project from the "Cricut" library and customize it.

So click on the "Projects" icon and type in "paper lollipop" in the search bar.

Step 3

Click on "Customize" to edit the project to your preference further, or simply click on the "Make It" button and load the cardstock to your "Cricut" machine and follow the instructions on the screen to cut your project.

Step 4

Using hot glue, adhere the down between the lollipop circles. Brush them with craft glue and sprinkle with glitter.

Paper Luminary

Materials

- "Cricut Maker" or "Cricut Explore"
- Standard grip mat
- Shimmer paper sampler
- Weeder
- Spray adhesive
- Frosted glass luminary

Instructions

Step 1

Log into the "Design Space" application and click on the "New Project" button on the top right corner of the screen to view a blank canvas.

Step 2

Let's use an already existing project from the "Cricut" library and customize it. So click on the "Projects" icon and type in "paper luminary" in the search bar.

Step 3

Click on "Customize" to edit the project to your preference further, or simply click on the "Make It" button and load the shimmer paper to your "Cricut" machine and follow the instructions on the screen to cut your project.

Step 4

Cut and weed the design, then spray the back of the shimmer paper with spray adhesive and adhere to the glass luminary, as shown in the picture below.

DIY Paper Marigold Flower

The Marigold flowers are used to decorate altars and graves, majorly in Mexico. This flower is popularly known as the flower of the dead. These beautiful flowers can be made in any color, and you could easily use this same technique for making a rich Mother's Birthday Day flower bouquet.

Items Needed For Paper Marigold:

- Scissors,
- 2 green pipe cleaners,
- A sheet of grift-wrapping tissue paper measuring around 20 by 26 cm. But it will be very nice if you purchase enough paper for a large quantity of dark yellow flowers.

How To Make It:

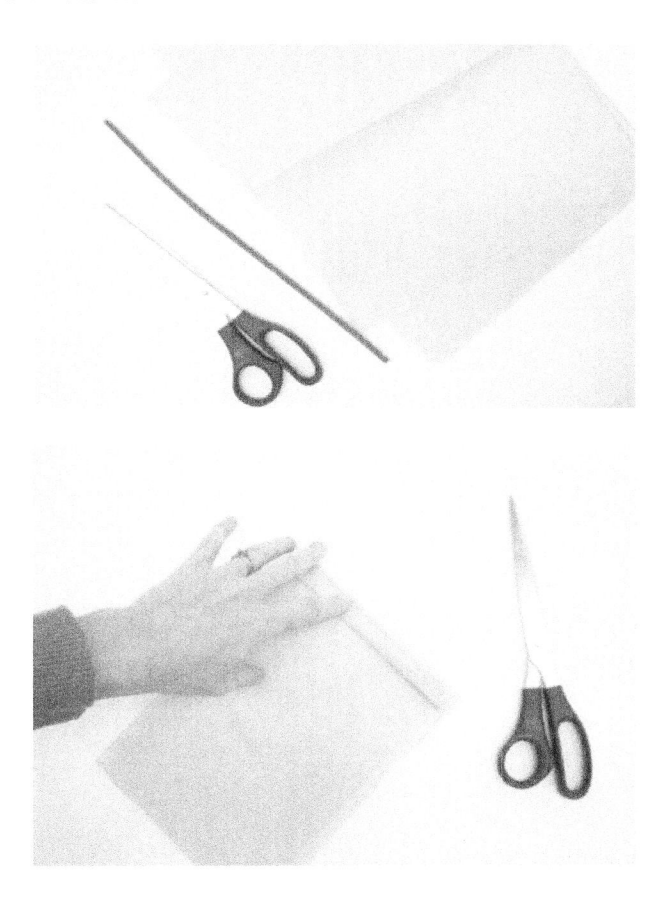

Step 1: Cutting the Paper

Cut the tissue paper by 1/2 to have 2 sheets each measuring: 13" by 20".

Further, cut each of the 2 pieces into half to give 4 sheets each measuring 10" by 13".

Go further to cut each of the 4 pieces into half to give 8 sheets of paper each measuring 7.5" by 10".

Step 2: Fold Then Cut the Paper

Pile up 4 sheets of paper

Plait the paper in an orderly manner

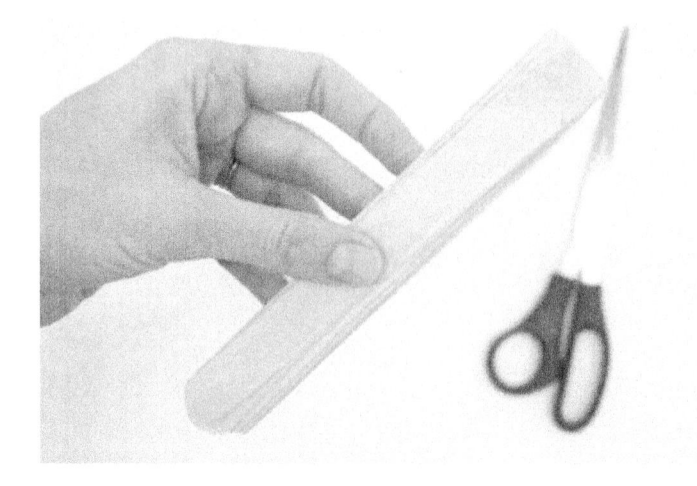

Cut a half-circle shape form each end

Wrap a pipe cleaner around the middle of the paper to hold it in place. This can also serve as the stem of the flower.

Step 3: Shape the Flower in a fan form

Fan out the paper

Slowly remove the first layers of paper from the remainder and take it up to form the upper layer of petals.

Slowly remove the rest of the paper layers

Puff out your flower

Continue by repeating these steps with the rest of the pile of 4 papers.

Display your Marigold Flowers

Magnetic Paper Flowers

Project thanks to My Sparkled Life

Adding a few bright flowers to your fridge can take your kitchen from average to extraordinary. It can help it go from a place you "have" to be to a place you "want" to be! You can create as many as you want, in any color or pattern that matches your décor. You can also come up with a variety of flowers to suit your mood or help you keep track of your family needs. They are also awesome gifts!

You'll need:

- Cardstock in a variety of colors or patterns
- Hot glue gun
- Magnets

Step 1

Open Design Space and develop the shape of your petals. These look good as half circles or oval shapes. You can also create bumped petal shapes by stacking oval over one another. Repeat the petal shapes to make enough flower magnets that you want. A large flower typically has about 12 petals, while a medium one has about eight. Medium petals are about two inches long, while large petals are usually about three inches. Measure the size of your magnet base and develop a circular flower base. You can add a small, ½ inch long slit at the end of every petal for the most comfortable construction if you want to.

Step 2

Once you have your petals designed and duplicated, load the cardstock on your cutting mat and get it ready to cut. Send the file to cut. If you did not add the slit in Design Space, use a crafting knife or an Exacto knife to cut a slit at the bottom of each petal. Once all the petals have a cut, add a dot of glue and glue one side to the other, making them into the petal shape. Do this to all the petals.

Step 3

Place your magnets down on the table and gather all the base circles and glue them to the tops of the attractions. Begin gluing the petals to the circle bases, starting on the outside and working your way in. Continue adding petals until it looks full. Large flowers will have about three or more layers, while the medium may only have two. Keep playing with your petals until you have a shape and set up that looks best to you. Leave a small space in the center of the flower open.

Step 4

Go back to Design Space and create smaller petals. Make them slightly smaller than the first petals. These are designed to add to the center of your flowers, so adjust them according to what you want. If you are unsure, try a few different shapes to try them out. Add the slits to the petals again, or wait until after they are cut to add the slits with an Exacto knife. When you are ready, send the file to cut. Create the petal shapes with a little bit of glue.

Step 5

Add glue to the flower design's interior and begin adding the smaller petals to the inside of your flowers. Gently pinch your flowers' edges for a more geometric appearance, or gently curve them inside for something more natural. You can add as many petal layers as you like.

Paper Succulents in a Container

Project inspired by The Happy Scraps

This pretty little project can be made to fit into any container you already have and can instantly add a little punch to your mantelpiece, table setting, or display. Make as many or as few of these different succulents as you want.

You'll need:

- Cardstock in teals and pinks
- Ink pads in different coordinating colors of teal and pink
- Sponges or dabbers for the ink
- Hot glue gun
- Foam to fill your container

Step 1

In Design Space, look for the design file for succulents. If you want to create the design yourself, make one large petal-shaped flower and then copy it about six times.

cale each copy down to a smaller size. If you need to, remove a petal or two to make it appear more proportional.

For the spiral and pointed succulent, make a spiral with three rings.

The center of the call should be a circle at the end. Add pointy triangles to the outside of the spiral lines.

Step 2

Once you have your designs ready, send your file to cut on your different colored card stock.

Remove your pieces and place corresponding flower pieces together on a covered work surface.

Using your sponges or dabbers, add a touch of ink to the outer edges of each petal shape or on the tips of the spikes of the spiral. You can keep the colors matching or contrast with a pink tip on a teal succulent and vice versa.

Step 3

Gently curl the edges of the petals up on the ends to make them more three-dimensional.

Step 4

Using your hot glue gun, glue the layers of the succulents together and roll the pointed succulents and glue them together as well.

Step 5

Place the floral foam inside your container, about ½ inch from the top. You can place your succulents on the foam or glue them down in the place where you like the arrangement. Once all your succulents are placed, consider covering the exposed foam with paper grass or shredded paper. You can glue this covering down if you like, but it typically looks best when it is loose.

Creative Herbarium

Learn how to dry your plants recovered in nature and collect them in your herbarium notebook or draw them in small drawing notebooks made yourself.

Materials

- Scandicraft Collection Herbarium Album
- Block of 24 assorted printed papers A4
- Assortment of 3 sheets of stickers
- Wooden press "My herbarium"
- Drawing pad A5 80 sheets - 90g - Monali
- A4 paper cutter
- Cricut maker

- Assortment of 3 washi tapes
- Fine black felt pen
- Double-sided adhesive tape - 6mm x 10m
- Sewing needle
- Sewing thread
- 1 pair of scissors
- Downloadable envelope and notebook templates

Instructions

1. Use of the press and the herbarium book 1. Collect fresh plants and flowers. Open the press to dry the plants. Take out the items: cardboard boxes, sheets of paper, and foam.

2. Place a sheet of thin paper on cardboard. Position the plant to dry. Cut back the stem if necessary. Cover with a second sheet of thin paper. In addition to this, you need to know more about it.

3. Stack the cardboard boards on top of each other. Place in the press. Cover the last plant with a thin sheet and cardboard. Add the mousses. In addition to this, you need to know more about it.

4. Close the press on the plants. Screw as far as possible to crush the plants. Leave to dry for at least a week, especially for plants that are thick.

5. Gently remove the plants and flowers from the press. Open the herbarium notebook. Place the flowers and plants in the chosen location. Maintain with a piece of washi tape from the

collection. Stick the rose with double-sided adhesive tape. Write the names of the plants. Stick a label to date the harvest and create a paper envelope to insert petals, seeds, etc.

6. Choose a paper from the collection. Fold in half crosswise. Measure 10.5 cm at the fold and cut with Cricut. Take 4 sheets of drawing paper. Fold them in half and cut them in the same way as for the blanket.

7. Mark the points to be drilled at the fold of the sheets using the template to download in Cricut. Pierce the leaves at the marks. Cut a sewing thread folded in 3. Pass the needle from the inside of the booklet to the cover. Bring the needle back to the center of the notebook and tie it at the fold. Do the same for each pair of holes.

8. Cut the sheets that protrude from the notebook using the cutter. Decorate the cover with masking tape from the collection. Choose stickers and glue them in the center to finish decorating the cover. In addition to this, you need to know more about it.

9. Your notebooks are ready to be filled with pretty dried plants or drawn during your walks.

CHAPTER 10:

Ideas with Clothing

Custom Graphic T-shirt

First, you will need to determine what you want your shirt to say. It is best to stick with just one color when you start. But as you get better at creating with your Cricut, you can move on to more color options in one design. Next is to pick which shirt you would like to use. This can be a preexisting shirt from your closet, or it could be one that you purchased specifically for this project. The shirt needs to be a material that can be ironed.

Supplies Needed:

- The Cricut machine
- Vinyl for the letters
- Your Cricut tools kit

I will walk you step-by-step on how you will make this vinyl lettering shirt.

1. Start by choosing the image you want to use. This can be done in Photoshop, or you can place your text directly into the Design Space.

2. Next, open the Cricut Design Space. Choose the canvas you wish to use by clicking the Canvas icon on the dashboard located on the left-hand side. Select the canvas that you will be using for your vinyl letters. This can be anything within the categories they offer.

3. Then, select the size of the shirt for the canvas. This is located on the right-hand side of the options.

4. Now, click Upload for uploading your image, which is located on the left-hand side. Select the image you are using by browsing the list of images in your file library. Then select the type of image that you have picked. For most projects, especially iron-on ones, you will select the Simple Cut option.

5. Click on the white space that you want to be removed by cutting out. Remember to cut the insides of every letter.

6. Next, be super diligent and press Cut Image instead of Print first. You do not want to print the image simply. You cut it as well.

7. Place the image on your chosen canvas and adjust the sizing of the image.

8. Place your iron-on image with the vinyl side facing down on the mat and then turn the dial to the setting for iron-on.

9. Next, you will want to click the Mirror Image setting for the image before hitting go.

10. Once you have cut the image, you should remove the excess vinyl from the edges around the lettering or image. Then use the tool for weeding out the inner pieces of the letters.

Now you will be placing the vinyl on the shirt.

1. And now, the fun part begins. You will get to iron the image on the shirt. Using the cotton setting, you will need to use the hottest setting to get your iron. There should not be any steam.

2. You want to warm the shirt by placing the iron on the shirt portion to hold the image. This should be warmed up for 15 seconds.

3. Next, lay the vinyl out exactly where you want it to be placed. Place a pressing cloth over the top of the plastic. This will prevent the plastic on the shirt from melting.

4. Place your iron onto the pressing cloth for around 30 seconds. Flip the shirt and place the pressing cloth and iron on the backside of the vinyl.

5. Flip your shirt back over and begin to peel off the sticky part of the vinyl that you have been overlaying on the shirt. This will separate the vinyl from the plastic backing. This should be done while the plastic and vinyl are hot. If you are having trouble removing the vinyl from the plastic backing, then place the iron back on the part that is being difficult. Then proceed to pull up, and it should come off nicely.

6. This should remove the plastic from the vinyl that is now on the shirt. Place the pressing cloth on top of the vinyl once again and heat it to ensure that it is good and stuck.

Although there are tons of steps, it is still an amazingly simple process.

Halloween T-Shirt

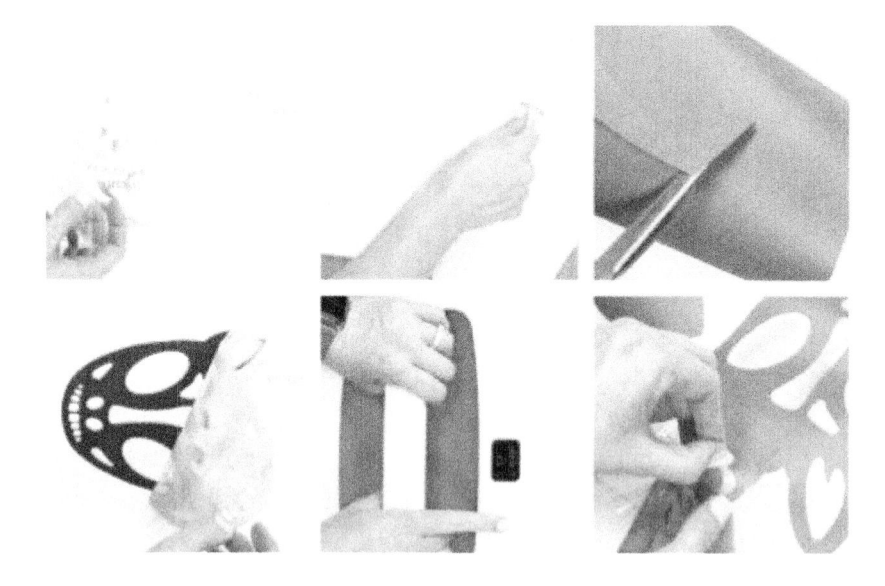

Materials Needed:

- T-shirt Blanks

- Glam Halloween SVG Files

- Cardstock

- Transfer Sheets (Black and Pink)

- Butcher Paper (comes with Infusible Ink rolls)

- LightGrip Mat

- EasyPress (12" x 10" size recommended)

- EasyPress Mat

- Lint Roller

STEPS:

- Import the SVG files into Cricut Design Space and arrange them as you want them on the T-shirt.

- Change the sizes of the designs to get them to fit on the T-shirt.

- Using the slice tool, slice the pink band away from the hat's bowler part (the largest piece). Make a copy of this band and then slice it from the lower part of the hat. With these done, you will have three pieces that fit together.

- You can change the designs' colors as you would like them. When you are done with the preparation, click "Make It."

- Ensure that you invert your image using the "Mirror" toggle. This is even more important if there is text on your design, as infusible ink designs should be done in inverse. This is because the part with the ink is to go right on the destination material.

- Click on "Continue"

- For the material. Select Infusible ink. After this, cut the design out using your Cricut Machine.

- With the designs cut out, weed the transfer sheet.

- Cut around the designs such that the transfer tape does not cover any part of the infusible ink sheet. Make sure that this is done well, as any part of the infusible ink that is not in contact with the fabric will not be transferred.

- Preheat your EasyPress to 385 degrees and set your EasyPress mat.

- Prepare your T-shirt by placing it on the EasyPress mat, then using a lint roller to remove any lint from the front.

- Insert the Cardstock in the t-shirt, between the front and back, just where the design will be. This will protect the other side of the T-shirt from having the Infusible Ink on it.

- If necessary, use the lint roller on the T-shirt again, after which you should heat your shirt with the EasyPress. Do this at 385 degrees for 15 seconds.

- Turn the part where the design faces on the T-shirt. Place the butcher paper on the design, ensuring, again, that the backing does not overlap the design.

- Place the EasyPress over the design and hold it in place for 40 seconds. Do not move the EasyPress around so that your design does not end up looking smudged.

- Remove the EasyPress from the shirt and remove the transfer sheet.

- To layer colors, ensure that your cutting around the transfer sheet is done as close as possible, then repeat the previous three steps for each color. This will prevent the transfer sheet from removing part of the color on the previously transferred design.

'Queen B' T-shirt

Supplies Needed:

- Plain cotton T-shirt in the color of your choice
- Iron-on vinyl, also called heat transfer vinyl (HTV, gold)
- Green Standard Grip mat
- Cricut Fine-Point Blade
- Weeding tool
- Pair of scissors for cutting the material to size
- Brayer
- Iron or the Cricut EasyPress Iron
- Cricut heat press mat to iron on

Instructions:

1. Start a new project in Design Space.

2. Choose **'Templates'** from the left-hand side menu.

3. Choose the **'Classic T-shirts'** template.

4. From the top menu, choose the type of T-shirt; kids short sleeve.

5. From the top menu, choose the size of the T-shirt; small.

6. The back and the front of the T-shirt will appear on Design Space in the workspace.

7. From the top menu, select the color of the T-shirt you are using; pink.

8. Select **'Text'** from the left-hand menu and type in **'Queen B.'**

9. Set the font; a great free font for this project is Bauhaus 9.

10. Position the text on the T-shirt, then set the size and change the color to gold.

11. Choose images and find a bee picture. There is a nice free image or some really cute images you can buy.

12. Position the bee above the B and set the color to gold. You can rotate it into a tilted position.

13. Click on the **'Make it'** button, and you will be prompted with another screen showing the design on the cutting board. This is because, for iron-on vinyl, you need to mirror the image. You mirror the image in order to iron it on with the correct side up. Click the **'Mirror'** button on the left-hand side of the screen.

You will see your writing and image look like it is back-to-front. You may want to move the bee over a bit, giving a bit of space between the image and writing.

14. Reset your dial on the Cricut to **'Custom.'**

15. In Design Space, choose the everyday iron-on for your material setting.

16. You can set the pressure to a bit more if you like.

17. You will see a warning letting you know that mirroring must be ON for iron-on vinyl. It reminds you to place the vinyl facedown as well.

18. Check that you have the fine-point blade loaded in 'Cartridge Two' of the Cricut. Nothing is needed for cartridge one.

19. Cut the vinyl to the space that is indicated by the Cricut Design Space.

20. Place the shiny side of the iron-on vinyl down onto the cutting mat. Use your brayer to smooth out the vinyl onto your mat.

21. Load the cutting into the Cricut, and when the Cricut is ready, click **'Go'** for it to cut.

22. Unload the cutting mat when it has been cut. Remove the design from the mat and gently remove the mat side of the vinyl from the carrier sheet (matte side of the vinyl).

23. Use the weeding tool to pick out the areas of the letters like the middles of the B.

24. Place your T-shirt onto the Cricut pressing mat with the middle section where you want the transfer to be.

25. If you are using the Cricut EasyPress, you can go to the Cricut website to find the heat transfer guide and the settings you will need for the press. Follow the instructions with the Cricut EasyPress.

26. For a normal iron, preheat the iron.

27. Place the Cricut heat press mat inside the shirt.

28. Heat the surface of the T-shirt for 5 seconds with the iron.

29. Put the design on the shirt where it is to be ironed on with the carrier sheet up.

30. Place a parchment sheet over the vinyl to protect the iron and the design.

31. Place the iron on the design and hold the iron in place on the design, applying a bit of pressure for up to 0 seconds.

32. Turn the shirt inside out, and place the iron on the back of the design for another 0 seconds.

33. When it is done, turn the shirt right side out and gently pull the carrier sheet off.

34. Do not wash the shirt for a few hours after the transfer has been done.

T-Shirts (Vinyl, Iron On)

To make custom t-shirts using your Cricut machine, you will need to use iron-on or heat transfer vinyl. Ensure that you choose a color that contrasts and matches well with your t-shirt.

Materials Needed:

- Cricut Machine
- T-shirt
- Iron on or heat transfer vinyl
- Fine point blade and light grip mat
- Weeding tools
- EasyPress (regular household iron works fine too, with a little extra work)
- Small towel and Parchment paper

STEPS:

- In preparing for this project, Cricut recommends that you prewash the cloth without using any fabric softener before applying the iron-on or heat transfer vinyl on it. Ensure that your T-shirt is dry and ready before you proceed.

- On Cricut Design Space, create your design or import your SVG as described in the section on importing images.

- If you are using an SVG file, select it and click on "Insert Images." When you do this, the image will appear in the Design Space canvas area.

- Then, you need to resize the image to fit the T-shirt. To do this, select all the elements, then set the height and width in the edit panel area, or simply drag the handle on the lower right corner of the selection.

- After this is done, select all the layers and click "Attach" at the bottom of the "Layers" panel so that the machine cuts everything just as it is displayed on the canvas area.

- You can preview your design using Design Space's templates. You access this by clicking the icon called "templates" on the left panel of Design Space's canvas. There, you can choose what surface on which to visualize your design. Choose the color of your vinyl and of the T-shirt so you can see how it will look once completed.

- Once you are satisfied with the appearance of your design, click "Make It." If you have not connected your machine, you will be prompted to do so.

- When the "Prepare" page shows, there is a "Mirror" option on the left panel. Ensure that you turn this on. This will make the machine cut it in reverse, as the top is the part that goes on to the T-shirt. Click "Continue".

- Next, you are to select the material. When using the Cricut Maker, you will do this in Cricut Design Space. Choose "Everyday Iron-On." On Cricut Explore Air, you select the material using the smart set dial on the machine. Set this dial to "Iron-On."

- Now, it's time to cut. To cut vinyl (and other such light materials), you should use the light-grip blue mat. Place the iron-on vinyl on the mat with the dull side facing up. Ensure that there are no bubbles on the vinyl; you can do this using the scraper.

- Install the fine point blade in the Cricut machine, then load the mat with the vinyl on it by tapping the small arrow on the machine. Then press the "make it" button. When the machine is done cutting the vinyl, Cricut Design Space will notify you. When this happens, unload the mat.

- With the cutting done, it is time to weed. This must be done patiently so that you do not cut out the wrong parts. Therefore, you should have the design open as a guide.

- After weeding, it is finally time to transfer the vinyl to the T-shirt. Before this, ensure that you have prewashed the T-shirt without fabric softener, as mentioned at the beginning of this project.

- To transfer the design, you can use the EasyPress or a regular pressing iron. Using a pressing iron may be a little more difficult, but it is certainly doable. Before you transfer, ensure that you have the EasyPress mat or a towel behind the material on to which you want to transfer the design so as to allow the material to be pressed harder against the heat.

- Set the EasyPress to the temperature recommended on the Cricut heat guide for your chosen heat-transfer material and base material. For a combination of iron-on vinyl and cotton, the temperature should be set to 330°F. After preheating the EasyPress, get rid of wrinkles on the T-shirt and press the EasyPress on it for about 5 seconds. Then, place the design on the T-shirt and apply pressure for 30 seconds. After this, apply the EasyPress on the back of the T-shirt for about 15 seconds.

- If you're using a pressing iron, the process is similar; only that you need to preheat the iron to max heat and place a thin cloth on the design, such that the iron does not have direct contact with the design or the T-shirt. This will prevent you from burning the T-shirt.

- Wait for the design to cool off a bit, then peel it off while it is still a little warm.

- Ensure that you wait for at least 24 hours after this before washing the T-shirt. When you do wash it, be sure to dry it inside out. Also, do not bleach the T-shirt.

Matching Family Disney Shirts

Project inspired by Travelling Mom

Maybe you are planning on going on a family vacation or planning a family photoshoot. Have you started looking at matching outfits yet? Have you freaked out over the cost of trying to get you all to look great together? As a Cricut owner, you do not need to suck it up and pay the cost. All you need to do is buy an inexpensive sweatshirt or t-shirt for every member of your family and design what you want for a fraction of the cost. For this project, you can make Disney themed shirts or any other image of your choosing.

You'll need:

- Cotton shirts for each member of your family or for each person you are making them for
- Iron-on vinyl in red and black
- Any additional embellishments you desire, like ribbon or glitter, etc.

Step 1

In Design Space, find the image of Mickey Mouse and aviator sunglasses. For the Minnie Mouse heads, add a bow shape to them.

Step 2

When you have your designs and words laid out for each shirt, send the file to cut. Make sure the heads and sunglasses are cut together from black iron-on, and the bows are cut from red.

Step 3

Most likely, you will need to use your weeding tool to remove parts of the design you do not want and then peel back the rest of the negative iron-on you do not want to show up.

Step 4

Heat your iron to the hottest setting and position your vinyl on your shirts. Test your transfer before peeling the backing off completely. Apply more heat as necessary to make sure the transfer is complete.

Step 5

When the iron-on has completely attached, peel off the plastic backing. Make sure to repeat the process for every shirt and design you made them for.

Easy Lacey Dress

Lace dresses are adorable, but they can be hard to get ahold of and difficult to make. Fake it without anyone knowing better using your Cricut!

The iron-on vinyl will look just like lace, and it will stand up to your child's activities much better than the real thing.

Don't limit yourself to children's clothes; add some vinyl lace to your own as well! White vinyl will look like traditional lace the most, you can do this in any color that coordinates with the dress that you have. Use a Cricut EasyPress or iron to attach the vinyl to the fabric.

You can use the Cricut Explore One, Cricut Explore Air 2, or Cricut Maker for this project.

Supplies Needed

- Dress of your choice
- White heat transfer vinyl
- Cricut EasyPress or iron
- Cutting mat
- Weeding tool or pick

Instructions

1. Open Cricut Design Space and create a new project.
2. Select the "Image" button in the lower left-hand corner and search "vintage lace border."
3. Choose your favorite lace border and click "Insert."
4. Place your vinyl on the cutting mat.
5. Send the design to your Cricut.
6. Use a weeding tool or pick to remove the excess vinyl from the design.
7. Place the design along the hem of the dress with the plastic side up. Add lace wherever you like, such as along the collar or sleeves.
8. Carefully iron on the design.
9. After cooling, peel away the plastic by rolling it.
10. Dress your child up in her adorable lacey dress!

Dinosaur T-Shirt

Everyone loves dinosaurs, and kids can't have enough t-shirts. Use iron-on vinyl to create the perfect shirt for your fossil-loving child! The small designs on the sleeves add a little extra, bringing it up a level from your standard graphic t-shirt. Just as with the rest of these projects, you can use the same idea with different designs. Customize a shirt for any of your child's interests. The Cricut EasyPress or iron will help you attach the vinyl designs to the t-shirt. You can use the Cricut Explore One, Cricut Explore Air 2, or Cricut Maker for this project.

Supplies Needed

- T-shirt of your choice
- Green heat transfer vinyl
- Cricut EasyPress or iron
- Cutting mat
- Weeding tool or pick

Instructions

1. Open Cricut Design Space.
2. Select the "Image" button in the lower left-hand corner and search "dinosaur."
3. Choose your favorite dinosaur and click "Insert."
4. Select "Image" again and search for "fossils."
5. Choose your favorite fossil and click "Insert."
6. Copy the fossil once so that you have two of them.

7. Place your vinyl on the cutting mat.

8. Send the design to your Cricut.

9. Use a weeding tool or pick to remove the excess vinyl from the design.

10. Place the dinosaur in the center of the t-shirt, and a fossil on each sleeve, with the plastic side up.

11. Carefully iron on the design.

12. After cooling, peel away the plastic by rolling it.

13. Show off the cool dinosaur t-shirt!

Conclusion

Congratulations! You reached this part, and that means you have been successful in your beginner's journey. Here are a few Cricut hacks to keep in mind:

- Keep crafting tools in one place

Collect the crafting tools and keep them in one place. It could be a box in which you can clearly see all the tools in one glance. Place it close to you so that they are easy to access when you need them. It saves you a lot of frustration when you are unable to find a certain tool and leave your project in the middle to hunt it in your craft room.

- Cover your cutting mats

Your Cricut mats come with a cover, so do not throw them away. Instead, use them to keep the mats dust free and clean between crafting.

- Keep extra blades

Always keep extra blades and tools handy. Whenever you feel that the blade is getting blade, replace it immediately with a fresh piece.

- Test cut on new material

This is important if you have never worked with Cricut materials or using a new one. So it is best to test the material by making a little cut on it, like a circle or a small heart.

By this, you will see the quality of the material, and you will know if you have chosen the right one. And you do not have to waste the whole sheet.

- Clean your Cricut mats

Besides covering the mats, they also need proper cleaning. You can always throw the dirty ones and replace them with the new ones. Until your mats turn non-sticky and greasy, clean with some cleaner. You can also use baby wipes to clean residue or grime on the mats.

- Always have good tools

Weeding tools are essentials, but along with them, you should also have paper trimmers and self-healing mats handy. A great Cricut tool that you must have is a True Control knife that will change your crafting game.

- Mirror Iron-on images

As mentioned in Cricut projects, you must turn on the mirror-on setting if you are working on an Iron-on material. Moreover, Iron-on has transfer paper, which you need to put onto your mat, shiny side down.

- Make your crafting activity a little faster

Cricut Design Space has a feature called "Fast Mode," and just like its name, it speeds up the process. Fats mode is a must if you want to be done with multiple projects quickly.

- Use sharpie pens

Cricut pens are amazing for personalizing your project. But when they run out, you can use less expensive sharpie pens in their place. They work well in the Cricut.

- Peel off the mat with gravity

To avoid curl in your Cricut paper projects, you need this hack! Peel the mat off your project by going with gravity, and you will see your paper project is perfectly straight.

- Replace scrapers with gift cards

Keeping scraper tools is a must in the craft room, but at times, you may not find them close to you.

Under this situation, reach out to your credit card and use it to smooth out the vinyl. You can also use old gift cards for this purpose.

- Always keep vinyl scraps

It is important to keep the scraps of vinyl as it does not grow on trees and are expensive.

So save some money by keeping the scraps and use them later in your projects.

You will be surprised to find that you can create lots of projects with vinyl scraps.

- Label your vinyl scraps

When you have collected the vinyl scraps, label them with a sharpie and then store them. This will help you remember the time when you stored the vinyl and for which project it was used.

- Weed on the mat

Another fun tip for weeding your design is to do it on the mat. This secures your design, and you can easily weed it.

- Keep weeded pieces

When you are weeding your projects, instead of leaving them in the working place, collect them in an emptied box like a tissue box.

This will not only keep your craft space clean, but it will also prevent the vinyl pieces from sticking to everything else.

- Keep painter's tape handy

You may want to wrap your hand when you are weeding. When you are weeding, you can stick the pieces to the take, and in this way, they will not end up in all of your working space. This hack is great when you are working on big Cricut projects.

- Reuse transfer tape

Yes, you can use the transfer tape again. So if you are a 4-by-4 piece of tape or similar pieces of tape with you, keep it for a couple of uses in future projects. Get maximum use out of it.

- Use spray adhesive to restick mats

When your mats lose their stickiness, tape off the edges, and then spray adhesive spray lightly on the mat. Let it dry, and then you will see that your mat is as good as the new one.

- Get an easy press

You need an Easy press, then which one will make your Iron-on process easier. It does not matter which one you should buy as they are all amazing.

- Keep some alcohol in the craft room

Alcohol will make it easier for you to work with slick surfaces. Just rub a little alcohol on these places, and you are good to go. You can also rub alcohol on mugs, plates, and glasses to wipe clean the fingerprints on them, and in this way, the vinyl will be able to adhere properly.

The next step is to experiment with your Cricut machine and all of the materials you can use with it. The projects in this book only cover a small portion of what the Cricut is capable of.

Tweak the ideas in this book to fit you perfectly. Change up the materials, the blanks, what the design is, and whatever else your imagination can come up with. Create your own projects, as well. Following the ideas in this book will give you a good foundation for using your Cricut. Once you've become familiar with it in the different ways that you can use it, you can let your creativity flow and create whatever you want.

For more inspiration, you can check out more books that are similar to this one or browse project ideas online. Cricut's website features a lot of project ideas, and the Cricut Design Space has some premade projects and templates that you can use. You could even join or create an online community for trading Cricut project ideas and swapping unused materials. Communities can be one of the greatest parts of crafting!

Cricut machines can produce shapes from 1" to more than 5" high anywhere. Simple to adjust metal cutting patterns, most styles of craft paper produce standardized shapes. These forms can be utilized to add custom letters, interesting borders, or festive shapes that represent any page's content. While many different card stock thicknesses may be used, scrapbookers should know that paper in a heavier grade might make the blades dull faster. This means that the sharpness of the blade should always be checked and replaced if appropriate in order to ensure good performance.

A Cricut computer is not a small investment. The prices start at about $100, and some people can not use this cutting machine. When considering, however, the costs of the production of pre-cut letters and forms, the computer will ultimately pay for itself, as are noticed by most committed enthusiasts. These may also be used for other documents, such as individual invites, gift tags, and holiday cards.

Printed in Great Britain
by Amazon